GARDENS, PLANTS and MAN

Ferns and birches, Dover, Massachusetts.

GARDENS, PLANTS and MAN

by
Carlton B. Lees

Executive Director
Massachusetts Horticultural Society

with original color photographs by the author
and
prints and plates from the rare book collection
Massachusetts Horticultural Society

A RUTLEDGE BOOK   PRENTICE-HALL, INC., ENGLEWOOD CLIFFS, NEW JERSEY

For George Hicks St. John
and all that he gave me when I was very, very young.

Fred R. Sammis	Publisher
John T. Sammis	Associate Publisher
Doris Townsend	Editor-in-Chief
Marilyn Weber	Managing Editor
Allan Mogel	Art Director
Norman Snyder	Designer
Therese Pol	Associate Editor
Jane Field	Associate Editor
Gwen Evrard	Art Associate
Arthur Gubernick	Production Manager

ISBN 0-13-346775-9
Copyright 1970 in all countries of the International Copyright Union by
Rutledge Books, Inc., and Carlton B. Lees

Prepared and produced by Rutledge Books, Inc.
Published by Prentice-Hall, Inc.
Englewood Cliffs, New Jersey
Library of Congress Catalog Card Number: 67–10531
Printed in Italy by Mondadori, Verona

Contents

Gardens are the link between men
and the world in which they live
for men in every age have felt the need
to reconcile themselves with their surroundings
and have created gardens to satisfy
their ideals and aspirations.

Sylvia Crowe
GARDEN DESIGN

And God said, Let the earth bring
forth grass, the herb yielding seed, and the
fruit tree yielding fruit after his kind,
whose seed is in itself, upon the earth:
and it was so.

GENESIS I:11

Preceding pages: Middleton Place, near
Charleston, South Carolina.

Introduction

The basic concept of this book was a long time aborning. I suspect that its beginnings were in earliest childhood, in the countryside, in Connecticut. The best part of that childhood was spent, summers, in a place called North Canton where roads were unpaved and automobiles were few. Plows, mowing machines and hay rakes were drawn by horses and the noises and smells of the internal combustion engine were uncommon. The air was clear and carried fragrances of fresh-mown hay, sweet-fern and autumn apples. Sounds were made by birds, livestock, wind and a lively brook. In addition, there was the continued excitement of my great-uncle's farm, of "The Kicker," a great Holstein who gave birth to twin calves on the Fourth of July, of new chicks pecking their way out of their shells and into the world, turning in a matter of moments from wet curiosities to fluffy buff-yellow delights. I suspect that I was a lonely child, but I never felt alone there.

The horticultural achievement I recall, not altogether with pleasure, was following my grandfather as he scattered seed potatoes in the furrows of his country garden. He gave me a stick 12 inches long and my job was to place the pieces, "eye" side up, exactly the distance apart dictated by the stick—and the line had better be straight, "by God!" It was tedious and I hated it. But I do remember the special flavor of tiny new potatoes, freshly dug, boiled in their jackets and awash in butter. And of sweet corn, not picked until the water in which it would be cooked was well on its way to boiling. Grampa was not altogether an unreasonable man.

My life became involved quite early with plants, in two ways: as horticultural problems and products, and as the whole and special world of farm, field and woodland.

It was not until many years later that I comprehended the idea—garden—in the sense of being a world, too. While I had learned to draw, to paint and to grow plants, it was not until I understood garden as the art which organizes outdoor space for man's use, comfort and pleasure that I accepted it as essential rather than as decoration.

The term *architecture* denotes the art form that has to do with building shelter for man, the shaping of indoor spaces for his use, comfort and pleasure. We seem to have no comparable term to apply to the shaping of outdoor space. Regional planning, urban renewal, landscape architecture, as terms, are inadequate. In centuries past, the garden as organized outdoor space often was given as much attention as indoor space, but at present the idea is too often restricted to cultivation, decoration and mere pastime.

The weakness of American gardening is the petunia-bed thinking of many who play a leading role in it, and a lack of understanding of it as environment. Man cannot continue to live in the ugliness he is perpetuating upon the land. If, as Henry Thoreau tells us, the preservation of the earth is in wildness, perhaps the preservation of man as a rational creature is in those portions of that earth which he occupies.

This book is not a statement only about gardens and plants. It is, I hope, much more.

Carlton B. Lees

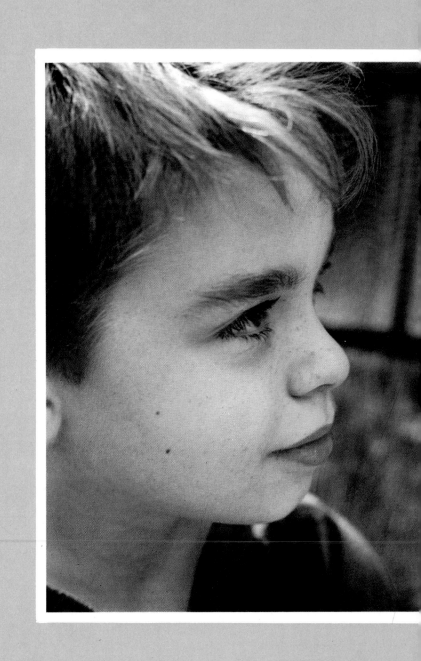

I. NONE ARE STRANGERS

Jane Brown Had a Problem

It had been a long, cold and grimy dark winter. The mortar and bricks of Jane Brown's world had gathered another coat of soot; it was dull, dark and depressing. She tried to close it all out with the lace curtains, but the drabness pushed itself in on her and set her mood every day.

Circumstance, being what it is, had placed Mrs. Brown in this neighborhood and in this tenement. She had always lived in the city, but something within her cried out for clean skies, bright meadows and cool forests and responded each year to the new leaves on the tree-of-heaven that grew in the alley.

Spring comes everywhere, to everyone, but to some it comes more clearly and with more assurance. Jane Brown recognized spring. She also recognized that hers was not a real world at all. Sun-colored buttercups and fragrant violets did not grow in her alley, and she could not do very much about it.

But she could grow a geranium. And she did.

Preceding pages: Author's son and hibiscus.
Above: Geranium in pot. Right: South End Alley, Boston.

The Royal Governor of Virginia was a gentleman; to him there was little that could not be accomplished through intelligent conversation and courtly manners. One was precise in choosing words, in dealing with people, in dress, in everyday living. A gentleman gave much attention to his surroundings: "3 dozen chairs, strong and fashionable . . . 2 large looking glasses with arms of the colony on them according to the new Mode . . ." (Governor's Palace inventory, Williamsburg, 1710).

From the world of post-Elizabethan London came such a man to build a palace in Virginia to house himself, his retinue, assemblies and "four hundred guests at supper." Governor William Gooch wrote, "The Gentm. and Ladies here are perfectly well bred not an ill Dancer in my Govt."

But, also, here was landscape untamed. Overabundant vegetation threatened the orderliness of palace life, so while the royal governor lived in a real world, it was too real for his comfort. It was without precision. So he brought order to the visual chaos of the Virginia forest by imposing his geometry upon it: severely clipped evergreens in obedient ranks, symmetrical patterns of boxwood, carefully pleached allées of hornbeam—reconciliation everywhere.

The royal governor did have a problem. He did not understand the forest; he feared it. He also knew that he could solve the problem in his way, according to his need, in his time.

And he did.

Although far apart in time, distance, culture and wealth, Jane Brown and the royal governor of Virginia were not strangers. Both created gardens as best they could within the framework of circumstance. While outwardly the visual results may seem very different, the basic need to link themselves to the world in which they lived was the same.

Sylvia Crowe speaks of men "reconciling themselves with their surroundings." The geranium that Mrs. Brown planted in her window box is mute evidence of this need. Why she planted the geranium she probably did not understand; the need was deeper than conscious understanding. She and the governor felt the pressures of their heritage, their common origin as creatures of the forest. While, according to Emerson, "nature hides every wrinkle of her inconceivable antiquity under roses and violets and morning dew," the antiquity is still there. We cannot escape the forest of our ancestry; the centuries we have traveled from Eden are a part of us.

City environments are artificial; they deny our origin. The frustrations we experience as urban people may well come, at least in part, from this denial, from not knowing who we really are. This is not to advocate the abolishment of cities and a return to the forest or even to the farm, but it does suggest that the great concentration of asphalt, concrete and steel of the Seattles, Chicagos and New Yorks of our world do not meet a most important basic need: to

Governor's palace garden, Williamsburg, Virginia.

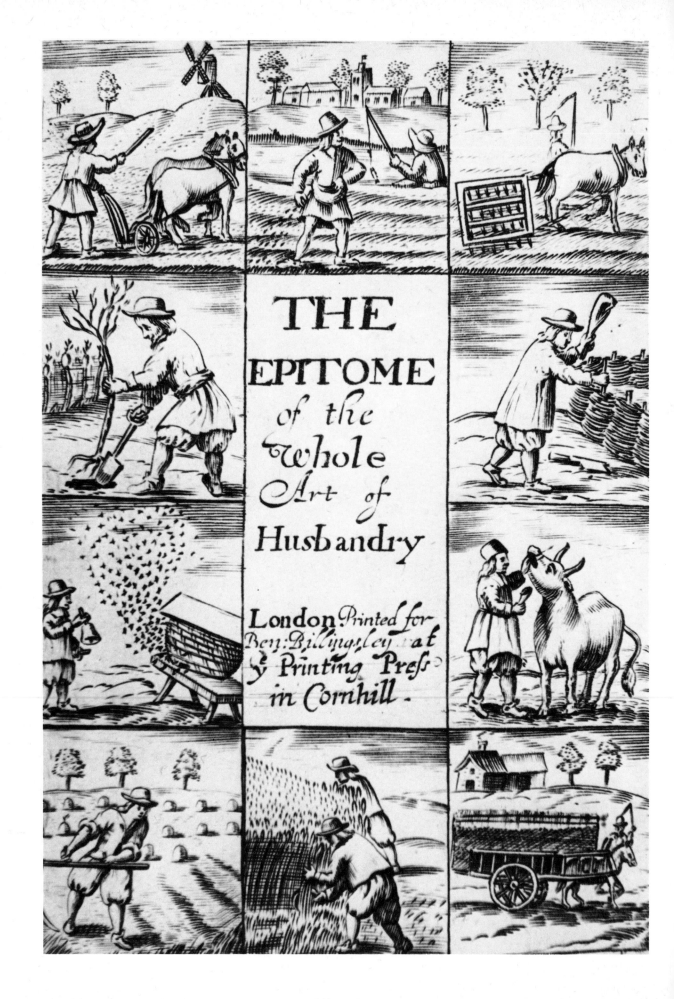

THE
EPITOME
of the
Whole
Art of
Husbandry

London Printed for
Ben: Billingsley at
y Printing Press
in Cornhill.

16

be at home in our environment. Recognition of this fact may well determine whether or not man as a species will remain a rational creature.

As cities sprawl across the land, the opportunities to experience natural landscape become fewer and fewer. Since man's very existence depends upon plants, it is essential that he have contact with them in order to recognize himself in the total scheme of things. "Many children today do not know where even a carrot comes from," states Bruce Gullion of the Massachusetts Department of Natural Resources, "and through not knowing, may grow up to destroy the very environment that sustains them."

Within the leaves of plants two inorganic compounds—carbon dioxide and water—combine to produce carbohydrates through a process called photosynthesis. This process is fundamental to all life; it is the one ultimate source of the food of the world. The carbohydrate manufactured in plant leaves is the body-building material for all living things; the complex metabolism of animal life is simply an elaboration or amplification of the primary products manufactured within that leaf.

The understanding of photosynthesis is very new in terms of the history of man. A beginning step was made with Joseph Priestley's discovery of oxygen and his observation that air in which animals could no longer live could be made to sustain animal life again if green plants were grown in it. Two years later, in 1774, a Dutch physician, Ingenhousz, reported that this purifying effect worked only if the plants were exposed to light and only if the green portions of the plants were used, but it was a Swiss, de Saussure, who found in 1804 that both water and carbon dioxide were absorbed in the process, that oxygen was liberated and that the plant tissue increased in weight.

In the process carbon dioxide of the air enters the leaf through stomata—tiny pore-like openings on the underside—and enters the spongy cells where it combines with water. This becomes possible with the help of a remarkable substance—chlorophyll—which is a complex protein composed of carbon, hydrogen, oxygen, nitrogen and magnesium. Chemically it is similar to the hemoglobin of the blood except that the latter contains iron instead of magnesium.

Chlorophyll, the green pigment of plants, is still something of a mystery. Light provides the energy necessary for its development, but questions about how it works are still unanswered. Two other pigments are closely associated with chlorophyll—carotene (red) and xanthophyll (yellow)—and may occasionally mask or hide the chlorophyll, as in the case of a red coleus leaf. If dipped in hot water, the red pigments of the coleus leaf are dissolved and the green of the chlorophyll becomes evident. In the bright red or yellow maple leaf in autumn the chlorophyll has ceased to exist; therefore the red and yellow pigments, usually hidden by the green, become conspicuous.

The product of photosynthesis is glucose, the carbohydrate which is the basis of all foods and from which, through the action of enzymes and by various chemical modifications, all other organic compounds of plants and animals arise. Other sugars and starches, closely related chemically, may also be produced. All are removed from the leaf factory for use in the growth of the plant and, fortunately for us, many are stored in seeds, fruits, tubers, enlarged roots and in other modifications of plant parts. A seed is a storage organ of food which is used to nourish the embryo plant as it develops, until it can put out roots and leaves and manufacture food to sustain itself.

The conspicuous starch-filled halves of a lima-bean seed emerge from the soil with the shoot and gradually shrivel as the stored food is used by the rapidly growing plant. The stored carbohydrate of the onion bulb nourishes the dormant plant within until the roots and new leaves develop sufficiently to sustain growth. The eyes of a potato sprout and grow even in darkness, nourished by the starch stored within the tuber, and will continue to grow without light until

Woodblock illustrations from the title page of New Additions to the Epitome of the Whole Art of Husbandry *by Blagrave, London, 1675.*

the stored food is completely used and the tuber shrivels to nothing. But the plant is not manufacturing food; it is only using stored food because, in the dark, photosynthesis is impossible.

Agriculture and horticulture, then, are concerned with the cultivation of large numbers of relatively few kinds of plants to provide food for ourselves, and began when the first man learned which seeds, roots and shoots to eat and which to avoid lest they taste bitter or make him ill. Although we eat meat and animal products, the cow and the chicken feed upon plants and change the basic plant food into meat, milk and eggs. The creatures of the sea depend ultimately on plants (chlorophyll-bearing algae) for their existence. Wool, leather, cellulose, oils, resins are ultimately the result of photosynthesis. The Brussels sprouts in the supermarket freezer are harvested from the land; so is the box that contains them.

So, while as strangers in the artificial city we need to experience the reality of trees and grass to remind ourselves of our place in the universal scheme, we must also remember that we are biologically dependent upon plants. The noted Brazilian landscape architect, Roberto Burle Marx, quoted in *Time* magazine, said, "It is obvious that the concept of a garden goes beyond an esthetic composition; it also signifies the necessity of men to live intimately with nature."

Mrs. Brown and the royal governor could not escape the forest from which they sprang, so entwined were they with it.

Preceding pages: Elm in winter, Hamilton,
Massachusetts. Opposite: Maples in autumn,
Topsfield, Massachusetts. Above: Elm in May,
Chestnut Hill, Massachusetts.
Below: Elm leaf, Bucks County, Pennsylvania.

Beech root on rock outcropping, Rye, New York.

Oak leaves, Swarthmore, Pennsylvania.

*That nature is out of date suggests
that what we think of as a love of nature
is a kind of fashionable sentiment.
The difficulty is that this is both true
and false. It is a sea of feelings,
psychic imagery, literary and poetic
insight, economic heritage, perceptual*
*habit, and other factors interwoven
with their own public and distorted
manifestations. Nature is real and love of
nature is part of its reality.*

Paul Shepard
MAN IN THE LANDSCAPE

Wild rose
in grass, Marblehead,
Massachusetts.

Spring woods, Lima, Pennsylvania.

... but there is no reason why I should dilate at greater length upon the pleasantness and delight of acquiring knowledge of plants since there is nothing in this life pleasanter and more delightful than to wander over woods, mountains, plains garlanded and adorned with flowerlets and plants of various sorts ... and to gaze intently upon them. ...

Leonhart Fuchs
DE HISTORIA STIRPIUM (1542)

Butterfly weed, Martha's Vineyard, Massachusetts.

Aster, Marblehead.

Preceding pages: Poppies and olive
trees, southern Spain. Left:
Christmas fern, Valley
Forge, Pennsylvania.

33

Cypresses in fog, Carmel, California.

Brook in
winter, Hamilton,
Massachusetts.

38   *Willow tree, Lancaster County, Pennsylvania.*

Monterey cypress trunks against the sea, Point Lobos, California.

We seem to make it our study to recede from Nature, not only in the various tonsures of greens into the most regular and formal shapes, but even in monstrous attempts beyond the reach of the art itself; we run into sculpture, and are yet better pleased to have our trees in the most awkward figures of men and animals, than in the most regular of their own. . . .

I believe it is no wrong observation, that persons of genius, and those who are most capable of art, are always most fond of nature; as such are chiefly sensible, that all art consists in the imitation and study of nature: On the contrary, people of the common level of understanding are principally delighted with the little niceties and fantastical operations of art, and constantly think that finest which is least natural.

Alexander Pope

Every artist, scientist, and philosopher
in the history of mankind has pointed
to the laws of nature as his greatest
source of inspiration: without the
presence of nature, undisturbed, there
would have been no Leonardo, no
Ruskin, no Nervi, no Frank Lloyd Wright.
    Peter Blake
    GOD'S OWN JUNKYARD

*Above: Crab-apples in sand dune, Ipswich,
Massachusetts. Left: Trees after ice
storm, Hamilton.*

Bald cypress, near Virginia Beach, Virginia.

Lythrum, Plum Island, Massachusetts.

View of lake, Blenheim Palace, Woodstock, England.

Under cherry-flowers
None are utter strangers
     Issa (1762-1827)
       HAIKU POEMS,
       ANCIENT AND MODERN

Japanese weeping cherry in winter, Beverly, Massachusetts.
Right: Same species in bloom, Wayne, Pennsylvania.

47

The Extraordinarily Good Citizen

In Philadelphia there exists an organization, called the Neighborhood Garden Association, which started in 1953 when a group of white suburban ladies plunged into the black slums with the idea that they were going to help people help themselves. The originator of this scheme was Mrs. James Bush-Brown, recently retired as head of the Ambler School, a rather nice if somewhat idyllic school for girls interested in horticulture and horses. Ambler was halfway around the world from the neighborhoods into which Mrs. Bush-Brown and her co-workers ventured. But the Quaker spirit of the Pennsylvania countryside is not easily daunted, and the least expected situation is met with no indication of displeasure or disapproval, and always with graciousness.

The ladies got the residents of a low-rent housing community near Poplar and 12th Streets, and another group of neighbors in West Philadelphia, to agree to take part in a project to erect and maintain window boxes on the sills of their dull brick houses. Somehow the men, women and children managed to put the boxes together and be ready for the soil and plants when they arrived. On the appointed day station wagons from such places as Swarthmore, Bryn Mawr and Gwynned Valley arrived with soil and with petunias, ageratum, geraniums, vinca and a myriad of other plants. It got a bit confusing and chaotic at times because most of the participants had no idea how to go about planting a petunia, much less taking care of it after it was planted. But the good ladies, with sleeves rolled up, per-

severed, and all was accomplished. Instructions were given for watering, and the ladies promised to return the following week to inspect the plants and give additional instruction.

Before the summer was over, whole blocks of Philadelphia were in bloom. Twelve thousand flowering plants were brought into neighborhoods and 427 window boxes were planted that first year. Sidewalks were swept, steps were scrubbed and the shabbiest of window frames were painted. Some blazed forth in beauty-shoppe pink and carnival purple, but they were clean and fresh. And bright. The neighborhoods had a new buoyancy about them.

Since that summer this story has repeated itself many times, over and over again, until now there are more than 500 garden blocks, 16 community gardens and 1,200 dooryard gardens in housing projects which are a part of Philadelphia's Neighborhood Garden Association. Each block has a leader and assistant leader and a dedicated group of workers. Each block receives assistance from the Association in the form of plants for three years only; then each is on its own. Bake sales, block parties, collections—all help each block group to raise funds for projects that have gone far beyond window boxes. On vacant lots, made available to the group by the city, have sprung up neighborhood gardens, tot lots and substantially equipped playgrounds.

As a result, where once there were grimy streets, new attitudes are evident. A young child may share his birthday cake at a party in a garden bright with zinnias where once there were only tin cans and broken bottles. A happy bride and her groom may receive wedding guests in a rose bower where yesterday there were junk automobiles. And when you talk to these people who have created and maintain these places within the confines of their own blocks and have given them such names as "Surprise Garden" and "Happiness Garden," they all end up saying the same thing: "We're neighbors again."

An awareness of belonging to the human race, of being a needed part of a larger group, of being able to do something and see the results—these are worth something, too.

From one lonely and dismal alley came the message that a woman wanted a window box. Mrs. Bush-Brown with an assistant picked her way through the litter to knock at the door of a particularly rundown row house. A large black woman appeared. Yes, she did want a window box. No, she had never grown anything before, but she had her fifty cents for the kit and promised to have it put together and ready for planting on the following Tuesday.

When the ladies arrived with soil and plants the owner of the window box, although extremely awkward at it, was encouraged to try planting and actually did succeed in getting the marigolds and petunias into the soil of the box without breaking them. She was told about watering, and what not to do as well as what to do. The box was ensconced on the sill of a dirty window backed by a ragged shade and the ladies departed, promising to return.

Another week passed, and when they arrived to inspect the window box its owner, very pleased with herself and filled with the excitement of two new blooms on the petunia plants, was waiting on the steps. The window had been washed. With a pair of scissors, someone had neatly trimmed the ragged edge off the window shade. As she stood there, beaming with her new success, the woman plunked her fat hands on her hips and exclaimed, "You know, Mrs. Bush-Brown, I'm going to get some tiebacks!"

Before summer passed, not only did crisp ruffled tieback curtains appear at the window, but the walls of the room inside had been washed. And on one September afternoon, when the window box was overflowing with the scarlet of petunias and the sunshine of marigolds, its owner warmed her teapot and put out bread and jelly in preparation for her weekly visit from the ladies who had brought the window box to her earlier that summer. High tea was enjoyed by three people who understood something about ideals and aspirations, and the need to reconcile oneself with one's surroundings. Neither did they underestimate the power of a petunia.

"Gardeners," said Barbara Ward at the White House Conference on Natural Beauty in May 1965, "make extraordinarily good citizens."

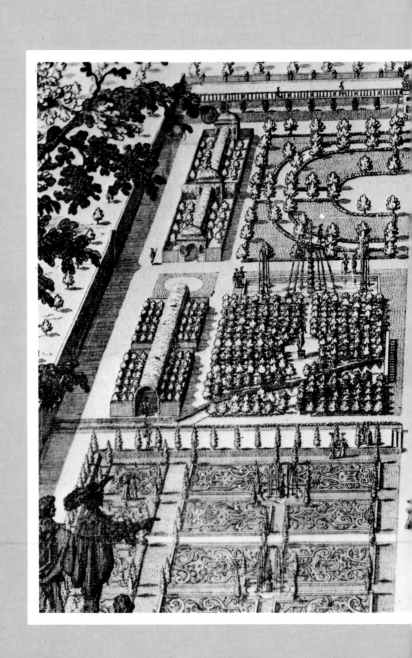

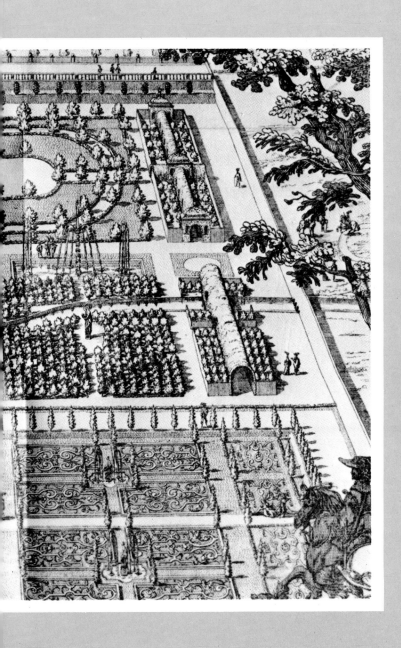

II. THE GREATER PERFECTION

Eden

Agriculture, it has been said, was the first act of civilization. But only an agriculturist would be guilty of so fraudulent a claim. Horticulture came before agriculture, and the garden itself came before both.

We doubt that man wandered aimlessly when he came down from the trees to live on the floor of the forest. Certainly he foraged for food, but he probably established some sort of home base very quickly. It might have been under the canopy of the tree itself or deep in a protective thicket, in the shelter of an overhanging bluff or cave. It is safe to suppose that very soon the landscape adjacent to and immediately surrounding this home base began to change. Probably he cleared away brush, gathered stones and contrived shelter from branches. When the first man organized this first bit of landscape, he created the first garden.

As man progressed, he gathered about him plants and animals which he recognized and knew he could depend upon for food. Learning how to grow plants may have come from so simple an act as the repeated spitting out of seeds and finding, after a time, plants emerging of the kind from which he had gathered the fruit originally. And so started the culture of the garden: *horticulture.* It was to be a long time before man was to progress to agriculture, the culture of the fields.

Garden is outdoor space organized for man's use, comfort and pleasure. The words *hortus, garden, orchard, yard* and *paradise* all have a common origin. All are concerned with the space immediately surrounding the domicile. The use of this space has two manifestations: (1) organization of landscape; (2) the growing of plants.

The Garden of Eden, opposite, is the frontispiece of John Parkinson's *Paradisi in Sole Paradisus Terrestris,* printed in London in 1629. Mr. Parkinson is neither more nor less guilty than every other illustrator of Eden: all have drawn it in terms of their own time.

J. C. Loudon, in his *Encyclopedia of Gardening* (London, 1802) states, "About the beginning of the seventeenth century, L'Adamo, a poem, was published at Milan . . . the prints . . . that are to represent paradise, are full of clipped hedges, square parterres, straight walks, trees uniformly lopped, regular knots and carpets of flowers, groves nodding at groves, marble fountains, and waterworks; and it is curious to contrast this representation of paradise with that . . . published in the present century; as, of course, each artist wished to represent what was considered most beautiful in pleasure-grounds at the time his picture was designed."

Mr. Loudon himself was not without prejudice, however, for he goes on to say, "Martin's picture, . . . as it represents a natural landscape, certainly seems best adapted to realise our ideas of Paradise. . . ."

While John Parkinson's garden hardly represents organized landscape, it is a delight to find in it such abundant variety, favorites that would be found in any horticulturist's Eden. Carnation and cactus, tulip, lily and pineapple all grow in harmony as, we suppose, all things should in Paradise.

Preceding pages: The garden at Wilton, England, created for the Earl of Pembroke by Isaac de Caus, 1615. From his Hortus Penbrochianus, reprinted in London, 1895. Right: Eden, title page of Paradisi in Sole Paradisus Terrestris by John Parkinson, London, 1629.

PARADISI IN SOLE
Paradisus Terrestris.
or
A Garden of all sorts of pleasant flowers which our
English ayre will permitt to be noursed vp:
with
A Kitchen garden of all manner of herbes, rooies, & fruites,
for meate or sause vsed with vs,
and
An Orchard of all sorte of fruitbearing Trees
and shrubbes fit for our Land
together
With the right orderinge planting & preseruing
of them and their vses & vertues
Collected by John Parkinson
Apothecary of London
1629

Qui veut parangonner l'artifice a Nature,
Et nos iarces à l'Eden, indiscret il mesure.

Le pas de l'Elephant par le pas du ciron,
Et de l'Aigle le vol par cil du moucheron.

The Ancient World

The gentle river which flowed out of deep Africa and into Egypt brought silt. With predictable regularity the river began to rise, overflowing its banks in July. Slowly and gradually it continued its flood through August and September; then quickly in October it would subside, leaving the silt upon the land. And in canals and reservoirs and ponds and garden pools the river left some of itself to help turn what otherwise would have been desert into rich, green valley. Trees of many kinds, agricultural crops, herbs, flowers and spices grew in profusion, all because of the river and the men who learned to live with it and use it.

The marvelous wall paintings of ancient Egyptian tombs provide a unique and comprehensive view of life along the Nile some 5,000 years ago. It was a sunny place, and the people had deep respect for the land as well as for the river. Great gardens were created for temples, avenues of trees were planted miles long, and private gardens were many. Rameses II is reported to have given more than 500 sites to temples for gardens. Groves of myrtle, olive, laurel and many other trees were grown, and medicinal herbs planted in temple gardens.

The private garden was walled to shelter it from desert winds and to conserve humidity. It usually was centered by a rectangular pool, from which small canals carried water to lesser pools. Thus was set the form of the garden, which was developed further with allées and groves of shade trees, rectangular plots of flowers, herbs, vegetables and fruit-bearing trees. Arbors supported grape vines and sheltered the occupants beneath. Cornflowers and poppies, mignonette, narcissus, acacia and tamarisk, dill, mint and caraway, jasmine and morning glory—bright color, delicate and lively fragrances and cooling shade—made paradise.

In the land known as the Fertile Crescent —a strip starting at the Persian Gulf and between the Tigris and Euphrates, reaching to the eastern shore of the Mediterranean— another civilization arose at about the same time as that of Egypt, but unlike Egypt it was without stone. The Sumerians, and later the Babylonians and Assyrians, built with sun-baked brick; with time it crumbled to leave only mounds above the plains where cities once stood. From the clay tablets of the period, however, much has been learned of the parks, hunting preserves, gardens and plants of those peoples.

On the broad plains bordering the two rivers, they also learned to irrigate their fields to grow onions, barley and groves of date palm. The date palm itself was of great importance because it provided wood for construction, leaves for baskets and matting, fibers, syrup and sap from which could be produced sugar and wine. Tender shoots, cooked, provided a vegetable, and in addition to the fruit being consumed in usual forms, a milklike drink was made from its juice. The most severe blow one could deal an enemy was to cut down his groves of date palms.

One of the brightest stories in the whole history of horticulture concerns the gardens that Nebuchadnezzar built on the plain of

Egyptian villa, from Les Jardins—Histoire et Description *by Arthur Mangin, Tours, France, 1867.*

Babylon, beside the Euphrates, to gladden the heart of his bride who missed the hills of her homeland. What a gift! Four acres of terraces rising tier upon tier, until there stood on that plain what must have appeared to be a huge verdant mountain.

According to Greek historians of the first century after Christ, each terrace was set back from the one preceding it, and all was supported by immense arches of the sun-baked brick.

Waterproofing was achieved with reeds, asphalt, tiles and large sheets of lead. On top of all this went the soil in which a large variety of trees, shrubs and flowering plants was cultivated. Cedars, larch, cypress, mimosa and palms—the largest of them were placed so that roots could penetrate into the hollow, soil-filled supporting columns below. Water was brought to the top, some say by ingenious mechanical devices but more likely it was by slaves, to keep this great mountain green. The waters of the Euphrates reached new heights of glory. From the top they fell to splash in pools below.

And while some historians dispute the very existence of the Hanging Gardens of Babylon, saying that the Greeks saw the remnants of only a fortress or possibly a ziggurat—a tall tower-temple symbolizing the link between heaven and earth—there are too many examples in later gardens to remind us of Nebuchadnezzar's gift. And if it had been but a ziggurat, what better link between heaven and earth than a garden, a very special ziggurat indeed!

Rome

Pliny the Younger (A.D. 62-113) was a gentleman of considerable education, wealth and culture, and he owned several particularly beautiful villas. Of one of these, Tuscum (plan opposite), he writes in a letter to a friend, "The land lies charmingly. Imagine a kind of amphitheatre, a broad spreading plain amongst mountains crowned with lofty and venerable forests.... Below this again stretch the vineyards right along the mountain side, making an agreeable line on the landscape. Then come meadows and cornfields.

"My villa commands as fine a view as if it were perched on the summit, and yet the ascent is exceedingly gentle. Behind stand the Apennines, far enough off for the intervening distance to soften the breezes blowing off them. The aspect is southerly, a broad and slightly projecting cloister catching the sun in the summer from the sixth hour onward—rather earlier in the winter. This cloister contains several apartments, with a hall after the ancient fashion.

"You descend to a sloping garden through an avenue of box trees cut, topiary fashion, into the shapes of animals....

"On the more level ground is a kind of sunk garden protected by a wall and a sloping bank, with paths enclosed by cut evergreen bushes and curiously shaped box plants. Then comes a lawn, rather formal in character, and fields further on, and coppices.

"Opposite the middle of the cloister is a pleasure or summerhouse built round a small courtyard with a marble fountain playing in the shade of four plane trees ... the fishpond lies immediately beneath, as charming to the eye as to the ear, while a waterfall breaks into foam with a delicious sound on the marble floor."

Of another garden, also at Villa Tuscum, he writes, "The moment you enter, you take it in at a glance—a space surrounded by plane trees covered with ivy, so that the tops of them are green with their own leaves and the lower portion green with the leaves of the ivy which creeps over the trunks and branches to form a perfect screen. Box and laurels are planted between, in order to intensify the shade. The garden runs in a straight line, broken at the end into a semicircle in order to vary design. A line of cypress forms a background. Within these are several inner circles in full sunshine, planted with roses to break the monotony of the shade with their brilliant colour.

"At the end of these winding ways the paths, enclosed by box hedges, run straight again. An expanse of lawn opens to the view, with box trees cut into a thousand shapes—sometimes in the form of a small pyramid, or letters to indicate the name or initials of the owner.

"At the end is a semicircular seat of white marble shaded by a vine supported by four small columns of Carystian marble. From the seat water gushes out of tiny pipes as if the weight of the person sitting there had put it in motion. The water is caught in a polished marble basin contrived so that it is always full without actually overflowing. My picnic basket and the heavier part of

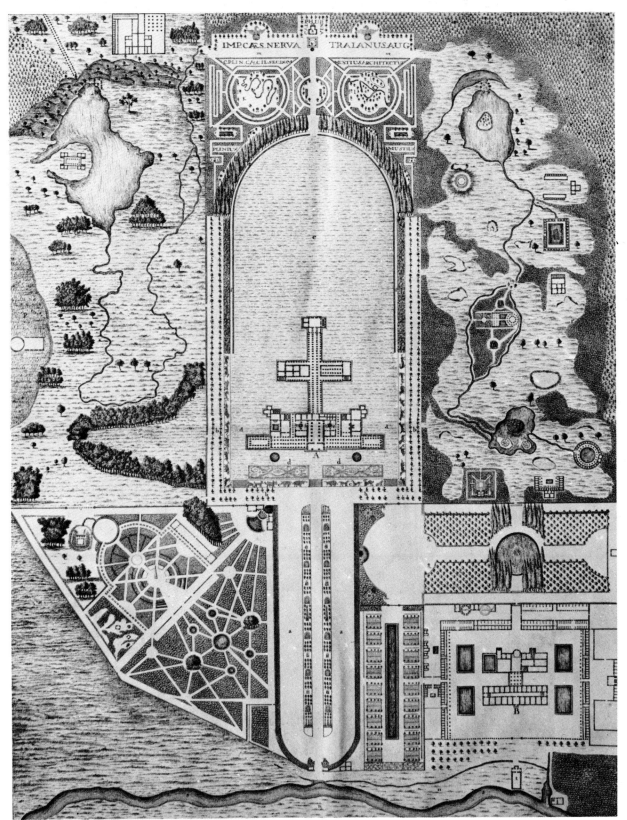

Plan of Tuscum. This was one of the villas belonging to Pliny the Younger, a first-century Roman statesman. His letters provide vivid descriptions of Tuscum and his other houses in Italy. This plan is an 18th-century reconstruction by Robert Castell, published in The Villas of the Ancients Illustrated, London, 1728.

my dinner service are put on the edge of this basin. The lighter pieces, made to resemble little boats and birds, float gently on the surface. On the other side a fountain throws the water high into the air in a spray and receives it again where the overflow runs out through a number of small orifices.

"Opposite the seat stands a summerhouse matching it in beauty, resplendent in marble, with doors and windows opening on to the shrubbery. A small retiring room is furnished with a couch, shaded by a luxurious vine which helps to keep off the glare. Here you lie as peacefully as in a sylvan grove. You can never get wet if it rains as you would in the open; and all the time a fountain is rising and disappearing.

"Dotted about are marble seats, with little fountains near them to welcome the tired walker. The whole length of the garden is refreshed by gurgling streams fed by pipes, which are also useful for watering the shrubs.

"One can retire there," Pliny continues

Above: Yew sheared to form a topiary bird, Blenheim Palace, England.

Left: Pliny's topiary zoo as illustrated in Les Jardins ... *by Mangin, 1867.*

"and be less interrupted. It is so snug and comfortable. You need not put on your best toga. Nobody comes to call on you. Everything is peaceful. . . ."

The Roman love for land was a high passion. Wealthy Romans owned several villas, large and small, anywhere from within daily commuting distance of crowded Rome to North Africa or some other faraway place in their vast empire. They were agriculturists at heart. Although they built a great city, they escaped from it to the country at every opportunity. Their love ranged from untouched natural landscape to rigidly sheared, purely ornamental plants (topiary). They are credited with being the first ornamental horticulturists, that is, the first to grow plants for beauty alone. While many beautiful plants appeared in many beautiful gardens before Rome, the theory has been expressed that the plants usually had a practical use: pot or medicinal herb, oil, fruit, aromatic or cosmetic value, dyestuff. It took the Romans to develop beauty for its own sake.

The concept of the villa is unique. It is not a house as much as a cluster of buildings and garden spaces in which it is impossible to separate indoors from outdoors. There were roofless rooms, gardens with walls, covered spaces without walls to let in the view and the fragrance of garden and countryside. The Roman's passion for trees, clipped shrubs and flowering plants, sun, sky and water directed him to make these elements an integral part of his living space. And he succeeded very well indeed, even to the point of developing the forerunner of the orangerie and modern greenhouse with windows of talc or mica in which roses were brought to bloom out of season.

The heritage of ancient Rome is evident today not only in the city itself but in the surrounding countryside and in small towns where even tiny balconies overflow with a brilliant abundance of plants of every kind, as if there were no such thing as enough and as if, without them, Romans as human beings could not possibly exist.

Canopus, *Hadrian's villa*

The Moslem World

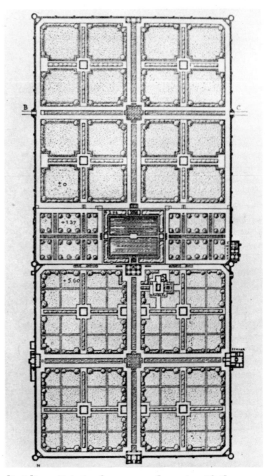

Rome was gone. In medieval Europe, knowledge of plants and gardens was cloistered inside monasteries, but a new prophet had been born in Mecca. He was to create an empire which by the eighth century would extend from India in the east, westward through Persia, Syria, Egypt and all of northern Africa to Spain. While the Koran taught that the religion of Mohammed should be spread by the sword, it also said that the Day of Judgment would take place in a garden of pleasure and that those favored to enter it would go to a verdant, shaded garden cooled by flowing springs.

In Persia the invading Moslems found the followers of Zoroaster who considered Heaven to be a garden with paths of burnished gold, with a pleasure pavilion of diamonds and pearls and filled with fruit and fragrant flowers. These concepts of Paradise were compatible with Islam, and as the Moslem empire grew, different cultures were absorbed, altered and blended. While the gardens of Persia and Spain were at opposite ends of the empire and thus not alike, neither were they totally dissimilar; they shared many characteristics.

The Persian garden was the result of three basic factors: climate, religion and love of green plants. In the windswept and often barren plateaus winter was cold, summer hot, so the garden became a miracle of spring and a protective oasis in summer.

For protection against wind and sun the garden was walled and thickly planted, and because of the need to irrigate efficiently, the garden was crossed by watercourses

dividing it into four equal parts. If the garden was large, the pattern was merely repeated so that the basic parts might be divided and subdivided by waterways. Where they intersected there was usually a pool. At the center of the garden might be the largest pool or a low hill upon which a pavilion was erected. The pavilion might be very small, seating only a handful of people, or it might be very large indeed, such as the one illustrated (page 63) in which a royal reception is taking place.

The structure of the pavilion was often richly decorated and hung. Pools and watercourses were usually tiled in blue (to create an illusion of depth) and often were beautifully rimmed and bordered with tiles of many colors. Still water was used for reflective quality, or it might move swiftly along a runnel from one pool to another. Often it

Preceding pages:
In ancient Roman
villas house and
garden were so
interwoven that
indoors and
outdoors could
hardly be
separated.
Remains of
colonnade and
canal at villa of
Hadrian, Roman
emperor, A.D.
117-138. Far
left: Plan of
garden at Lahore,
India, is typical
of gardens
of Islam.
Illustration from
Indische Gärten by
Marie Luise
Gothein, Berlin,
1926. Left:
Evening reception
in Isfahan,
imperial city of
Persia (1598).
Drawing by
Engelbert Kaempfer,
published in his
Amoenitatum
Exoticarum,
Lemgoviae (modern
German name:
Lemgo), 1712.

Court of the Myrtles, the Alhambra, Granada, Spain.

was sent upward in slender and graceful jets so that it cooled the air and added its musical splashing sound to the garden. Because images were forbidden by the Koran and by earlier Persian religious codes, sculpture and statues were not a part of these gardens. This fact is significant in establishing the manner in which water was used and is one of the basic differences compared to later European gardens where sculpture was used so freely in pools and fountains.

The Persians resorted to flowers for color and fragrance, and the music of birds, stringed instruments and voices in song were added to the water sounds. The cypress, representing death, and the plum or almond, symbolizing life and hope, were necessary to every garden. Most of the flowers were local wildlings brought into the garden, but Persia is the home of narcissus, tulips, grape hyacinths, lilacs, wallflowers, larkspur, hollyhocks, of jasmine and carnations and of lilies and roses of many kinds. Since "Each morn a thousand roses brings," as Omar Khayyam said in his *Rubaiyat*, the Persians had little need for imports.

As the Moslems spread across Egypt and as their African converts, the Moors, reached into Spain, the garden evolution continued. Plants from the east were carried westward and plants from the west traveled eastward. In Africa and Spain there were ruins of Roman villas. Again local needs—protection from heat, wind and sand —directed the development of living space, indoors and out. Indoor spaces were made to open into a courtyard or patio. This became garden surrounded by building. That the concept of the patio, the Court of the Lions at the Alhambra or the cloister of European monasteries might derive from the Roman peristyle is not inconceivable.

There stood in the foothills of the snow-covered Sierra Nevada in the south of Spain an ancient fortress called the Alhambra (red castle). It dominated Granada. About 1238, four centuries after the Moslems had come to Spain, Mohammed ben Alhamar began to build a palace within its walls. As a result, the Alhambra has become one of the garden treasures of the world. That the stone lace of the palace and the brute mass of the fortress fit so well together is startling, and when the mass and the lace are reflected together in the marvelous mirror pool of the Court of the Myrtles the effect is enchanting. This beautiful court gets its name from the hedges of myrtle that border two sides of the large pool.

The Court of the Lions at the present is almost entirely paved and is planted with but a few small orange trees. It is thought that it once abounded with flowering plants. The stone lions, supporting the bowl of the central fountain from which the court takes its name, are contrary to the laws of the Koran, and their origin is in dispute.

Across a small valley from the Alhambra is a lovely retreat, the Generalife. Its Court of the Pool is within the original Moorish section, the slender arched water jets and long narrow watercourse echoing the gardens of Persia far to the east.

Court of the Lions, the Alhambra.

Court of the Pool, the Generalife, Granada.

Medieval Gardens

What has been termed "an unaccountable phenomenon," the Middle Ages, descended upon Europe after the collapse of Rome in the fifth century. The darkness was to last nearly a thousand years, until the Reformation and the invention of printing rekindled the light in the 15th century. During this period a rigid feudalism discouraged change. Towns were walled; castles and manors were moated. Serfs were bound to their landlords, and if they did not live within the walls of the town or castle, their huts and houses were clustered close to the walls so they could seek safety inside in time of danger. Because of this, gardens became something quite separate from living spaces; they existed outside of the walls and the moat. Only medicinal plants were grown inside, available during sieges and other times when the gates were closed.

Medieval gardens developed patterns and shapes and characteristics that were peculiarly their own, independent of any relationship to indoor living space. One literally went "out" to the garden—outside the walls. The geometric patterns, the use of fences, of seats, of mounts and sundials, of edging materials for flower beds—all were to leave their indelible mark on gardens to come for centuries after. In the dooryards of New England, in the town-house gardens of the South and the cottage gardens of the British Isles we can still see these influences.

Medieval gardens were of two basic types: the herb garden and the orchard or pleasance. Herb gardens were essentially kitchen gardens and included potherbs,

Medieval towns and manors were walled and moated for protection. Space was at a premium so gardens existed outside the walls. Illustration from Architectura Curiosa Nova by Georg A. Böckler, Nürnberg, 1664.

medicinal or physic herbs, poisons (for dealing with enemies) and love philters. The latter were thought to make a person fall in love and were given much importance.

It was the monks inside the monasteries who kept plant knowledge alive during this long period. They exchanged plants and plant information with other monasteries and orders during crusades and pilgrimages. Medicinal herbs were grown, harvested and cured in quantity and dispensed at the monastery gates, so while prescribing and dispensing prescriptions, the monks cared for bodies as well as souls.

Because medieval gardens were not within the dwellings as in ancient Rome, Persia and Spain, they developed their own patterns, with many flowers, ornaments and fountains—the only places for women's outdoor recreation. Decorative panel from title page of Tabernaemontanus, Neuw Kreuterbuch, Frankfurt, 1588-1591.

Flowers were an important part of medieval gardens, valued for their fragrance and color. Illustration from Hortus Floridus, *by Crispijn van de Passe, Utrecht and Arnheijm, 1614.*

The pleasance, or pleasure garden, was just that. It was not meant to be great art or impressive or awe-inspiring or even a mark of status. It was a place where one could find pleasure in the shade of trees, surrounded by the color and fragrance of lawn and flowers. These gardens were the only outdoor spaces available to women, so dangerous was the countryside at large. These gardens tended to emphasize delicacy.

The "flowery meade," for example, was a flower-strewn plot of grass and was valued as a strolling (and lolling!) place. Indeed, so much pleasure was derived from sitting directly on the turf that raised benches with turf seats were constructed with wattle (woven fencing) to hold the sides. The word orchard, which we use for designating a grove of fruit-bearing trees, originally was applied to a grove of trees planted only for shade and often included a flowery mead beneath the sheltering branches. Sometimes it was used for describing the whole garden.

If we try to imagine ourselves pulling up the drawbridge each night, moated for protection and huddled within the walls in times of siege, it is easy to accept and understand the almost frivolous lightheartedness of these gardens. And if in our time not enough people give gardens the importance they were given in ancient Rome, in Renaissance Italy, in 17th-century France and in 18th-century England, perhaps we should remember that the Middle Ages after all lasted nearly a thousand years. They, too, are a part of our heritage.

New Dawn in Italy

By the 12th century, Europe was moving out from under the shadow of the Middle Ages, and in the mid-15th century a new and radiant light dawned in the form of the Italian Renaissance. Towns and cities flourished; trade grew, and with the exchange of goods came the exchange of ideas. But the real seeds of this renewal were in the rediscovery of the ancient civilizations of Greece and Rome, the study of which turned man's major interest from religious matters to the more worldly problems of everyday living.

The renewed trade brought wealth, so it also was a time of generous patrons who valued and supported the arts and financed the continued search for knowledge. Not least of these patrons was the Church of Rome. It was a time of rare scientific and superb artistic achievement, of great painting, great literature, architecture and sculpture, a period in which some of the greatest gardens of all history were created. While the Italian Renaissance is considered to have lasted, at the very most, 300 years, the extraordinary brilliance of its light warms us still in the 20th century.

Pliny's descriptions of his villas, rediscovered, had considerable influence on the Renaissance architect. The garden was no longer an afterthought, as it had been in the Middle Ages, but came to be conceived as an integral part of living space. As the architect moved out into the landscape it became easier to cope with uneven terrain. Instead of the gentle sloping plains with broad vistas prized by their ancient Roman ancestors, Renaissance men sought hillsides that pro-

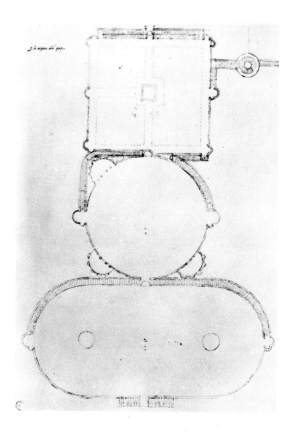

vided both the challenge and the opportunity for spectacular handling of the land contours in an architectural manner. Indeed, the Villa d'Este is more nearly a vertical experience than a horizontal one, so steep is its site. When Raphael chose the slope of Monte Mario for the Villa Madama, he set the tone for the great villas to come. Although the villa was never completed, Raphael intended to unite house and garden space as never before, making one inter-

Raphael's plan (opposite) for the Villa Madama, overlooking Rome. While he began it in 1515 and never finished it, Raphael nonetheless established hillside terrains as sites for villas to come. (Plan reproduced in Italian Gardens of the Renaissance by J. C. Shepherd and G. A. Jellicoe, Ernest Benn Limited, London, 1925.) Left: Casino and gardens of Villa Farnese at Caprarola were designed by the architect Vignola. Palace is on foundation of old fortress and was started in 1550; the casino, even higher on the hillside, was built after Vignola's death.

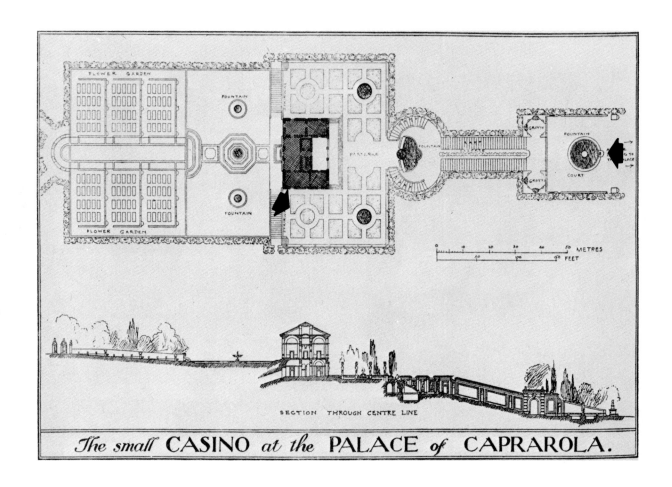

The small CASINO at the PALACE of CAPRAROLA.

SECTION THROUGH CENTRE LINE

locking unit of closely integrated parts.

The two most important gardens of the early Renaissance—the pre-baroque best of it—are within a dozen miles or so of each other and are credited to an architect named Vignola. They are the Villa Farnese at Caprarola (sometimes referred to simply as Villa Caprarola) and the Villa Lante at Bagnaia.

The Villa Lante is a small jewel of rare perfection that sparkles with special brilliance in the afternoon sun of the Italian sky. While most historians consider it the finest of the Renaissance gardens, some consider it the finest of any vintage, anywhere in Europe.

Villa Lante dates back to the late 15th century when a nephew of Pope Sixtus IV enclosed the wooded area above the town of Bagnaia to create a hunting preserve. A

later cardinal, Giovan Francesco Gambara, developed the garden and built the first *palazzina*, which was completed in 1578. After the death of Cardinal Gambara (then a bishop) in 1587 the villa passed through several owners until, by 1623, it was completed and looked much as we see it today.

Through the centuries, Villa Lante continued to be a favorite summer place for cardinals, popes and kings who were entertained here until early in the 20th century. After several decades of neglect and World War II damage, careful and respectful restoration brought the villa again to its early 17th-century condition.

It has been said of the Villa Lante that its fame is earned by perfect moderation. It is very small when compared to other important gardens of the period. Others have richer detail. It is not particularly architec-

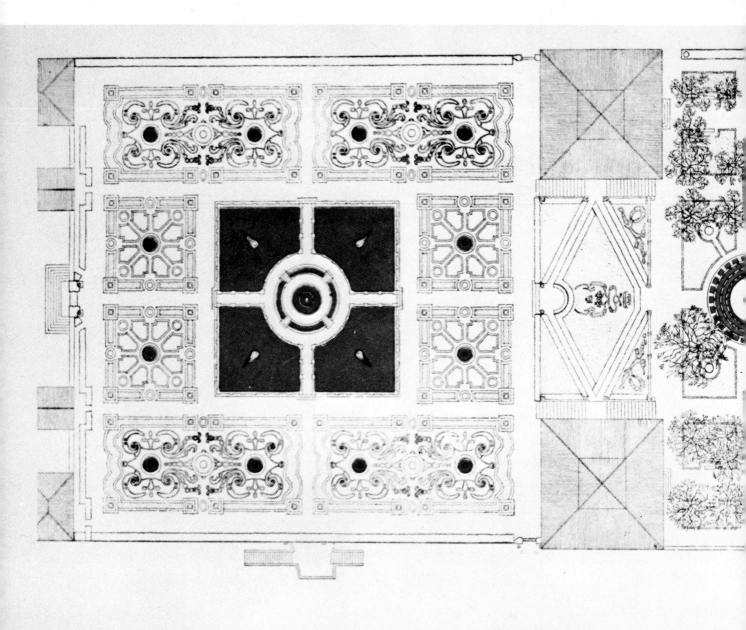

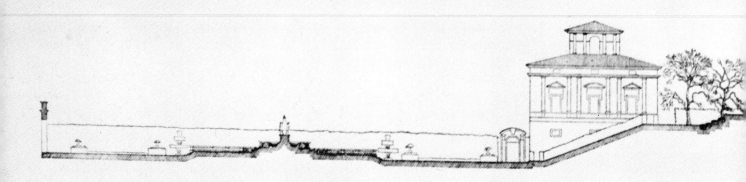

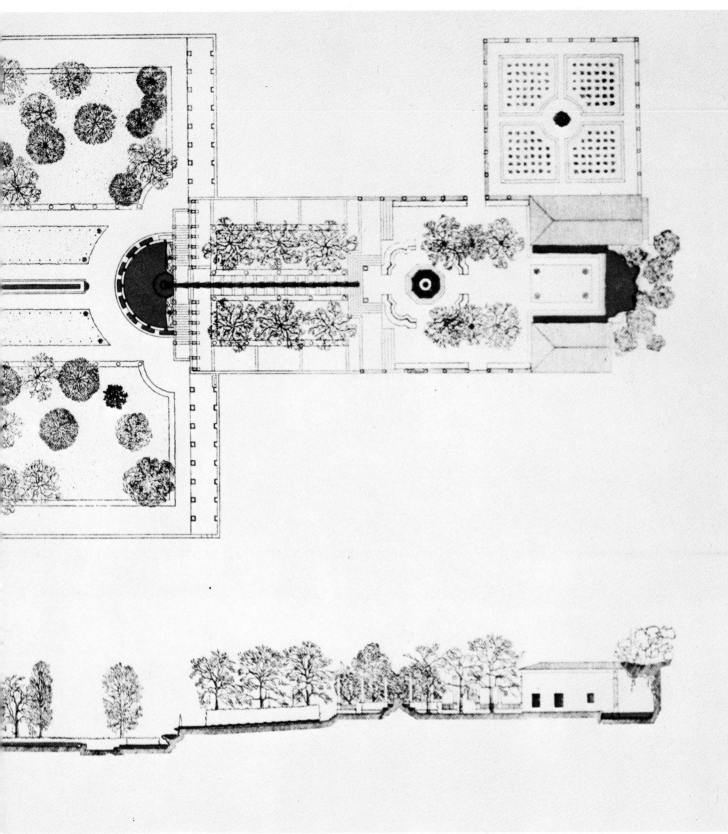

Plan, Villa Lante, Bagnaia. Vignola is
credited with the design of this garden,
considered to be not only the outstanding
garden of the Italian Renaissance but one
of the finest of all time.

Plan reproduced by special permission,
Francesco Fariello, Architettura dei
Giardini, Edizioni dell'Ateneo, Rome,
1967. Succeeding pages: Lower parterre,
Villa Lante.

tural in character. The view from the garden is of the rooftops of the town, not a distant or spectacular vista. Its only real advantage over the many fine villas of Rome is its natural woodland and its abundant water supply. While the latter is used generously it is not made a spectacle and fits well into the garden.

But the perfection is overwhelming. It makes one realize that here is a garden that grew first of all from an imaginative and carefully thought-out plan; and, secondly, although construction required nearly a century, that the plan was respected throughout. The result is a balance of elements—architecture, sculpture, water, sheared and natural plants—which is comfortable, pleasurable, exciting and completely comprehensible.

To visit Villa Lante is to experience perfection.

If Villa Lante is "perfect moderation," then Villa d'Este must approach perfect ostentation. When Cardinal Ippolito d'Este II was appointed governor of Tivoli in 1550 and bought an old Benedictine convent attached to the church of Santa Maria Maggiore, he pulled out all the stops. Here probably the most spectacular of the early villas of the Italian Renaissance was created. The architect, Pirro Ligorio, put together for the cardinal such a monumental ensemble of fountains, jets, cascades, pools, ponds, waterfalls, sprays and gurgles that even in the brilliant sunlight of 20th-century high noon Villa d'Este seems more fantasy than reality.

After one recovers from the initial impact, the coherence of this garden becomes evident. The site is very steep, but the sensitive and ingenious use of it leads to many surprises and to swift changes of pace from one vista to another and from one level to another. If Villa d'Este is not a small perfect jewel, it has nonetheless a kind of perfection that has to be measured in another way. Perhaps it is a matter of scale. If the Wall of One Hundred Fountains were only fifty, it might be plain dull. The small gurgling basins lining the Steps of the Boiling Sound are enchanting because of their extreme individual simplicity and great number. The Fountain of the Dragons, whether you gaze up at it or down upon it, is an impressive jet in any man's terms. And the effervescence of the Fountain of the Ovàto, where the playful imagination of the architect provided a walkway under a waterfall, is sheer P. T. Barnum, but Barnum with high style.

Bright though the midday sun may be, the refreshing vitality of the Villa d'Este is irresistible; it is a sensual, gleeful, place.

Right: The Villa d'Este, Tivoli, is built on an extremely steep hillside overlooking Hadrian's villa. This view of the central axis, from the Round Place of the Cypresses, only hints at the great vertical dimension of the garden (see plan, page 83).

Fish pools, Villa d'Este.

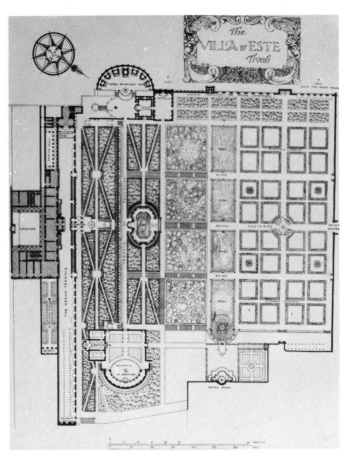

Plan, Villa d'Este, built by Cardinal Ippolito d'Este, after he was appointed governor of Tivoli in 1550. Designed by Pirro Ligorio. Reproduced from Triggs, The Art of Garden Design in Italy, *1906.*

Fountain of the Ovàto, Villa d'Este.

In France: The Grand Manner

When Charles VIII, who reigned from 1483 to 1498, retreated from his attempt to claim the kingdom of Naples and first brought Italian artisans and *objets d'art* to beautify his castle at Amboise, he sowed the seeds of the Italian Renaissance in France which were to germinate, flourish and eventually produce that spectacular bloom of the 17th century that came to be called "The Grand Manner." Its brightest flower among many bright flowers was to be Versailles, the creation—and creator—of Louis XIV.

The evolution between the castle of Charles VIII at Amboise and Versailles required more than 150 years. His immediate successors, Louis XII and Francis I, also fostered the Italian influence by bringing Renaissance artisans to France. An engraving of Louis XII's castle at Blois reveals how the new patterns were made to fit into the medieval character of the walled and moated structure. Francis I was a builder; he enlarged Blois and later built Fontainebleau. Among the Italians he commissioned to France was Leonardo da Vinci. By the time that Nicholas Fouquet built Vaux-le-Vicomte in 1650, the influence of the Italian Renaissance in France had undergone the evolution necessary to create something completely and distinctly French.

The basic differences between terrain and purpose necessitated constant adaptation of the Italian idea to make it work in France. The villa was a summer country house whereas the castles and chateaux of France were lived in all year around. The villas of Italy were built on the sides of hills, but

Preceding pages: Grotto designed by Bernard Palissy, most famous grotto builder of 17th-century France. From Mangin, Les Jardins . . . , 1867. Above: Garland of roses, primulas, viburnum and other flowers in marble, at Versailles.

By the mid-17th century castle walls were no
longer needed for protection. The house
illustrated (from Böckler, Architectura
Curiosa Nova, 1664) is so similar to Vaux-le-
Vicomte that at first glance it is easy
to mistake it as such.

most of the land of France where the court and its aristocracy were centered was flat. Instead of water moving rapidly—tumbling, splashing and jetting—the French had to use water in still, flat surfaces, mirroring the sky, chateau, sculpture and bosquet. Where the villa could be charming and intimate and at the same time provide openings into distant views from its hillside location, views in the French flat garden had to be created and controlled. Hence the development of the exceedingly long main axis bordered by forest. It forced the eye to see it all almost at once. The reaction of the viewer was to gasp, exactly as was intended.

Where the Italian garden of the early Renaissance even in its architectural extreme could be delightful and comprehensible, the 17th-century French garden became a conscious, bigger-than-life statement which at first glance appears to be almost coldly intellectual. Fortunately, however, as is true with so many first impressions, this one does not stand for long.

Vaux-le-Vicomte set the pattern for the culmination of the French garden in Versailles. Nicholas Fouquet bought three villages and pulled them down to make space for this marvelous chateau and garden which he conceived as a stupendous stage for the important business of entertaining and impressing important people. It was to be an elaborate setting for an elaborate society, and when Fouquet hired Louis Le Vau as architect, Charles Le Brun as interior painter and designer and André Le Nôtre as garden designer, he put together an excep-tionally competent team which was to set a new pace for houses, gardens and parks.

Vaux-le-Vicomte echoes the perfection of Villa Lante. The garden is almost entirely revealed in the first glance, the bordering woodland limiting the side movement of the eye and forcing it down the long axis of broad terraces gently dropping toward the valley of the Anqueuil (a small river channeled into a formal canal crossing the main axis), then up the long allée to the giant statue of Hercules silhouetted against the sky. But what at first appears to be coldly measured symmetry turns out to be rich with subtle and interesting variation always designed to emphasize the oneness of the overall scheme. Elaborate? Not really; perhaps because of the vast scale, what might seem elaborate at first glance (e.g., the parterre) fits as it should into the overall scheme and the illusion (or truth) is one of simplicity and exquisite taste.

Louis XIV was invited but did not attend the opening fête at Vaux, was furious when he heard such glowing accounts of it and, after attending another party given there in his honor (and at his suggestion), had Fouquet thrown into prison where he remained until his death 19 years later. The money for building Vaux? Well, Fouquet was superintendent of finances for all France—even the king himself found it necessary to consult him on money matters. Could be that the king was justified. Besides, as Cardinal Wolsey demonstrated when he presented Hampton Court to Henry VIII, the servant should never outshine the master.

The great boxwood parterres at Vaux-le-Vicomte
are only four to six inches in height. Central axis
extends through parterres, down subtle changes
in level, across canal and uphill.

View, garden from within the chateau of Vaux-le-Vicomte.

The team which built Vaux-le-Vicomte—Le Vau, Le Brun, Le Nôtre—moved on to Versailles at the bidding of Louis XIV to create what was to become the ultimate statement for the French garden. It was also to create a king unquestioned, an absolute monarch, who was to play so superb a role on this most magnificent of stages that before the century ran out he would be known as *Le Roi Soleil,* the Sun King.

The Versailles of Louis XIII was. a small chateau that was used as a hunting lodge. After seeing Vaux-le-Vicomte, Louis XIV in 1661 seized upon his father's simple lodge as the nucleus for his new palace. By 1668, seven years later, the garden façade had expanded to 1,325 feet in length and the small garden had grown to include 250 acres. But the palace and garden were only a part of the transformation; a town had to be built to serve the palace. By 1682, 20,000 people were gathered at Versailles.

Out of swampland, André Le Nôtre created a garden of staggering proportions to meet the requirements of this royal pageant. The. main axis extends three-quarters of a mile from the façade of the palace to the beginning of the Grand Canal. The canal itself then carries the axis to the horizon. As if this were not enough, the secondary axis, which crosses the immense terrace centering the garden front of the palace (and above which, indoors, is the Hall of Mirrors), also terminates spectacularly. On the north is the Basin of Neptune and on the south, across the Orangerie, the large lake of the Swiss Guards. Countless intersecting

In 1661 Louis XIV decided to use his father's chateau at Versailles as the basis of his new palace. Its gardens became perhaps the most famous in the world. Above: View of Louis XIII's chateau, from Mangin, Les Jardins . . . , 1867.

Versailles: The Tapis Vert leads from the upper terrace to the canal in the far distance.

Versailles under construction. The architect
was Le Vau, the garden designer Le Nôtre. From
Mangin, Les Jardins . . . , 1867.

walks, paths and subaxes lead to countless
secret gardens hidden away amid the woodland which, when viewed from the palace
terrace, appears to be dense and uncompli-
cated except for the provocative openings
into it.

Although Louis XIV built Marly, Clagny,
the Trianon de Porcelaine and the Grand
Trianon, Versailles continued as the focal
point of the court for half a century. During
that period many changes were made, but
only in detail, and the basic garden as originally conceived and carried out by Le Nôtre

in the initial development (1661-67) remains.

That Versailles escaped the strong de-
structive emotions and acts against the sym-
bols of absolute monarchy, during and after
the French Revolution, is something of a
miracle. Or perhaps the miracle is Versailles
itself. Although the long reign of Louis XIV
(1643-1715) has been referred to as the Age
of the Sun King, it has been suggested that
it be more correctly called the Age of Fouquet in honor of the man who set the tone
for it at Vaux-le-Vicomte while Louis was
still young.

Fountain of Flora and woodland allée at Versailles.

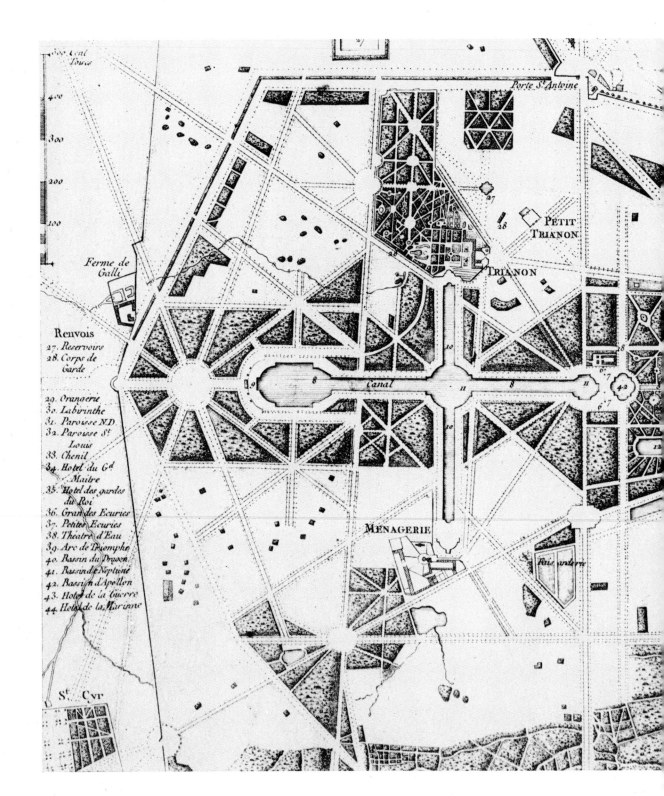

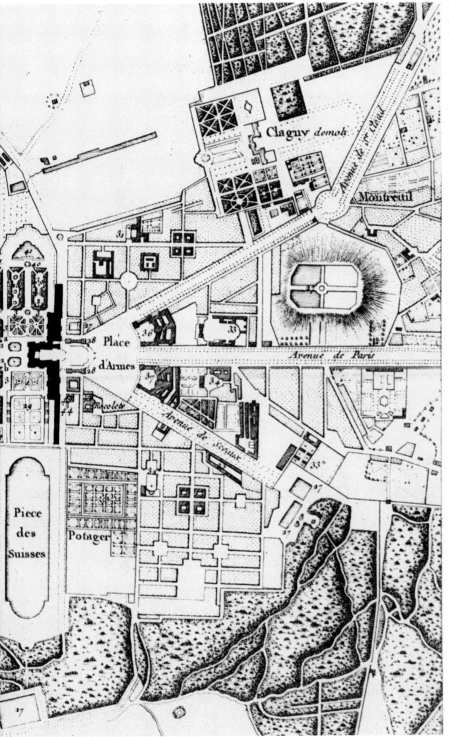

Plan of park of Versailles. Note size of palace (which was occupied by 5,000 people) in relation to entire park. Distance from palace to beginning of Grand Canal is three-quarters of a mile. From Le Rouge, Des Jardins Anglo-Chinois, Paris, 1776.

View from water parterre, Versailles.

Basin of Neptune and allée leading to north parterre and palace.

Neptune, water parterre, palace of Versailles.

Above: South parterre overlooking Orangerie and Lake of the Swiss Guards, Versailles. Right: Parterre de broderie at Champs, once the residence of Madame de Pompadour, near Paris. Opposite: Parterre often became so elaborate (parterre de broderie) that plants were few. Designs were carried out with boxwood or other low-growing evergreen combined with aggregates of various colors (coal, crushed brick, gravel) and lead edging. A plan from Dezallier d'Argenville, La Théorie et la Pratique du Jardinage, Paris, 1709.

Marly with its detached guest houses and elaborate hedges was also built by Louis XIV, not far from Versailles, as a retreat from palace life.

Petit Portique pour l'entrée d'un bois

Grand Portique de Treillage

Cabinet de Treillage percé à jour.

Niche avec Buffet d'eau

Salon Servant d'entrée à un berceau

The plans for trelliswork were elaborate, but in gardens of sheared tree walls and high hedges they served as entranceways and façades, emphasizing the architectural quality of the sheared plants. From Dezallier d'Argenville, La Théorie et la Pratique du Jardinage, *1709*.

Treillage at Marly. Unfortunately the architectural painted-wood latticework of the period was too fragile to survive. From Mangin, Les Jardins . . . , *1867*.

"Knowle," the manor house of Charles Sackville. I. Knyff, Britannia Illustrata, London, 1749.

"Pleasant Delytes," Perfection and the Victorians

When Francis Bacon wrote his essay on the ideal garden, he made a plea for the garden as an organized unit. He had seen the results of the ostentation of Cardinal Wolsey and Henry VIII at Hampton Court where the medieval idea was merely elaborated upon until it became a collection of overdone decorative elements more appealing to the fancy than the imagination, a garden of "Pleasant Delytes."

Bacon allowed no leeway in his ideal garden; it was to be of specific size and layout. Nor did he hesitate to damn parterres and other features of which he disapproved. The area he prescribed was 30 acres divided into three parts. The first part was similar to Le Nôtre's terrace immediately adjacent to the garden façade of the palace of Versailles, but Bacon insisted that this section should be nothing but lawn, ". . . because nothing is more pleasant to the eye than green grass finely shorn." Where Le Nôtre might have parterres, Bacon says, ". . . as for making knots, or figures, with divers coloured earths, that they may lie under the windows of the house on that side which the garden stands, they are but toys. . . ." He did provide for walks, hedged and covered with trelliswork, down each side of the lawn so that in hot weather one might pass in comfort to the second section of the garden.

This second section consisted of 12 acres, was square and surrounded with alleys of hedge and trelliswork, above which there were to be turrets for bird cages or ". . . broad plates of round coloured glass, gilt, for the sun to play upon." And in the middle of this most elaborate of the three sections he calls for a "fair mount" 30 feet in height. This is a distinct holdover from the medieval gardens and reminds us of Henry VIII's mount at Hampton Court.

The third section of Bacon's ideal garden was to be a wild garden with thickets of honeysuckle and the ground bright with strawberries, violets, pinks and primroses. In a sense this is an attempt to create idealized natural landscape, something the English were to do with perfection a century and a half after his essay.

Although he insists that each of the three basic parts of his scheme should be sufficiently separated from each other so that a view is allowed into each as it is entered, Bacon's plan does not encompass the concept that all three might be linked in some way to provide a continuing vista.

While Francis Bacon revealed Renaissance thinking in his appeal for organized landscape, he reminds us, ". . . it [the garden] is the greatest of human pleasures; it is the greatest refreshment to the spirits of man, without which buildings and palaces are but gross handiworks." This may ring of the Renaissance but it still separates house from garden. The English never approached the concept of Raphael's Villa Madama or Pliny's Tuscum, in which building and garden were closely integrated. Even in the great 18th-century park landscapes, where house and garden might be uniquely suited to each other, it is too often easy to imagine any of a number of great houses in settings of other great houses. To attempt such an

What Road more entertaining Lies than This,
Yet none Leads more direct to HAPPINESS.
Ja: Gardiner.

The Italian Renaissance helped shape English gardens in the early 17th century. Villa Lante was completed when the Pilgrims landed at Plymouth (1620) and Cardinal Wolsey's Hampton Court passed into the hands of Henry VIII in 1629. By the 1700s French garden influence had grown strong in England. Illustrations (left), Rapin, Of Gardens . . . , 1706, and Charles Evelyn, The Lady's Recreation, London, 1717.

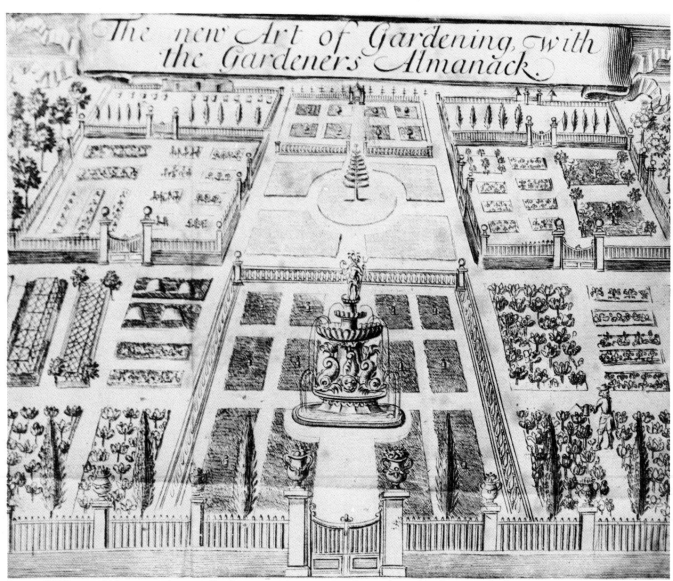

In 1688 William and Mary came from Holland to rule England and English gardens were influenced by Dutch ideas. The gardens of Colonial Williamsburg, Virginia, were created in this period and reveal Dutch influence, which is also echoed in the above illustration from Leonard Meager, The new Art of Gardening . . ., London, 1697.

illusion at Villa Lante, Villa d'Este or Vaux-le-Vicomte is impossible.

Lest this be considered critical of the English garden, I hasten to add that the natural landscape of England is after all more beautifully suited to occupancy by man than those of France and Italy. It is a kinder landscape given to gentleness of contour, color and season. Wild flowers are not limited to spring, and grass stays green all summer long. Hardwood trees reach magnificent proportions and impressive outlines quite unaided by man. The Englishman has always been able to turn to his countryside for spiritual refreshment; perhaps in England there is less need to perfect the garden as an exercise of the intellect.

Bacon's essay did help bring to an end the garden of the Middle Ages and encouraged sophistication. In 1615, Isaac de Caus created a garden for the Earl of Pembroke at Wilton (pages 50-51) which echoes Bacon's essay almost precisely.

Wilton was to become the most advanced garden, and the most admired, in England. Three quarters of a century after it was started, John Aubrey wrote, "King Charles I [reign: 1625-49] did love Wilton above all places and came thither every Sommer."

The French influence introduced into England at Wilton was to grow, especially as the famous family of French professional landscape gardeners—the Mollets—arrived to work on St. James Park in mid-century. One of the family had been appointed gardener to James I before 1625. Under James I and Charles II Hampton Court began to

break away from its Middle Age patterns. The *patte d'oie,* the goosefoot pattern of allées, radiated outward to establish a relationship between the palace and its vast park. These radiating allées were to appear again and again in English gardens and while they remind us of Versailles, they are earlier and were due to the influence of the Mollet family rather than that of Le Nôtre.

When William and Mary came from Holland to occupy the throne of England (1688), Christopher Wren designed the south addition to Hampton Court and the great parterres were added to the semicircle at the base of the radiating allées. With them came the Dutch influence on gardens. This hardly could be considered a step forward because Holland did not achieve new concepts as did France, Italy and, later, England. Because land in Holland was restricted in area, flat and crisscrossed by irrigation ditches and canals, gardens were small and rectangular. There were no vistas, so the Dutch tended to miniaturize what they saw in Italian and French gardens and to crowd topiary, parterre, sundial, sculpture and fountain together.

The result suggests a box of very fancy bonbons (which should be sampled one at a time, not by the boxful). Yet with the excesses removed, the Dutch gardens were to set a pattern for town gardens in particular, not only in England but in America, too. One has only to venture to Colonial Williamsburg, the gardens of which owe far more to Holland than to England.

The long allées at Hampton Court, as they

reached out into the park, gave an inkling of what was to come. By the end of the 17th century the taste makers of England were in an uproar: Sir William Temple, Joseph Addison, Alexander Pope. Pope on topiary: "Adam and Eve in yew . . . St. George in box, his arm scarce long enough but will be in condition to stick the dragon by next April." In the mid-18th century Horace Walpole was to write in retrospect, "To crown these impotent displays of false taste, the sheers were applied to the lovely wildness of form with which nature has distinguished each various species of tree and shrub. The venerable oak, the romantic beech, the useful elm, even the aspiring circuit of the lime, the regular round of the chestnut, and the almost moulded orange-tree, were corrected by such fantastic admirers of symmetry. The compass and square were of more use in plantations than the nurseryman. . . . Trees were headed, and their sides pared away; many French groves seem green chests set upon poles. . . ."

Of French symmetry, Pope scornfully observed,

"—each alley has a brother,
And half the garden just reflects the other."
Of the Dutch taste, Walpole in his essay *On Modern Gardening* continues, referring to the "boxed-in" series of gardens at Lady Orford's, "This, like other silly fashions, which, begun without meaning, are frequently continued with as little, lasted down to the reign of King William, and fell in with the mechanic taste of the Dutch."

Luckily, according to Walpole, "At that moment appeared Kent, painter enough to taste the charms of landscape, bold and opinionative enough to dare to dictate, and born with a genius to strike out a great system from the twilight of imperfect essays. He leaped the fence, and saw that all nature was a garden—his rulling principle was that Nature abhors a strait line."

William Kent—architect, painter, furniture designer, interior decorator, garden designer—was one of a long list of extremely able men who were to idealize the natural landscape and create a new concept for gardens. Kent is generally credited with making the first break with the established pattern. He banned canals, basins and fountains in favor of water in more natural form, "to serpentise seemingly at its pleasure." By this time, Hogarth's "curve of beauty" was drawing-room conversation; that it should be applied to landscape as well as to other arts is not unreasonable. It was Lancelot "Capability" Brown who carried the English park to its perfection, wiping out the formal gardens that came before him and bringing his idealized landscape right up to the walls of great houses which once looked out upon parterres, allées, basins and fountains.

So it came to be. England in the 18th century did rid itself completely of foreign garden undercurrents, turned to its own landscape and refined it to such sophistication that it came to be what we expected all England to look like: gentle meadows, clusters of the most noble trees imaginable, glorious lakes so ingeniously created that to think of them as man-made was sacrilege.

No other landscape concept has had so great an impact upon America. With the industrial revolution came great money and the creation of a new but unlanded gentry. When vast estates were being assembled and built on Long Island and in Grosse Pointe, the new gentry turned to England for patterns that were copied well into the 20th century. But perhaps even more significant is this influence upon public parks all across the United States. From Boston to Seattle, there are hundreds of parks in the tradition of Kent and Brown.

New York's Central Park, smack in the middle of a skyscraper city, is a direct descendant of the idealized English landscapes that preceded it. It is less obvious in design than the geometric, intellectual exercise of the Tuileries and is really quite un-self-conscious. Central Park appears to have happened all by itself; yet perhaps its contrast to the geometry of the city is the very thing that makes it work. Our inheritance is not a meager one.

Lancelot "Capability" Brown carried the 18th-century English park landscape to its zenith. Any object that suggested it might not be a part of the natural landscape was removed or concealed, and while to the untutored eye it might appear that these were informal landscapes they were in fact highly formalized. Their formality had much in common with Japanese gardens; the error is to confuse formality with geometry.

Brown and André Le Nôtre were possibly the two greatest talents of all garden history, but Brown is often credited with being

Tudor or Pond Garden and William II's Banqueting House, Hampton Court.

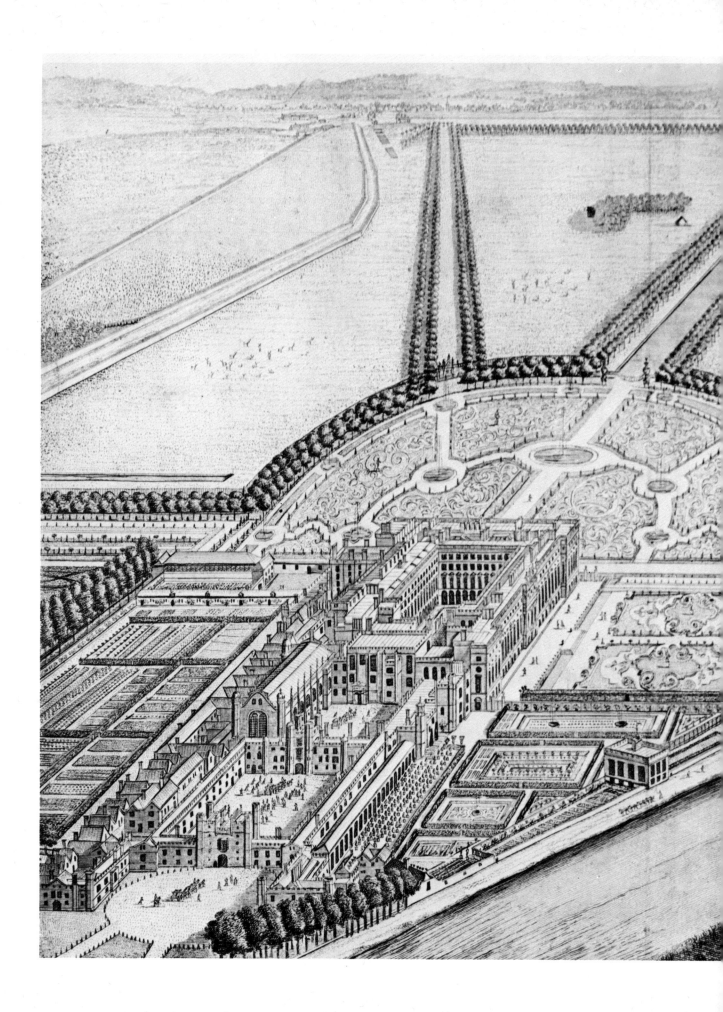

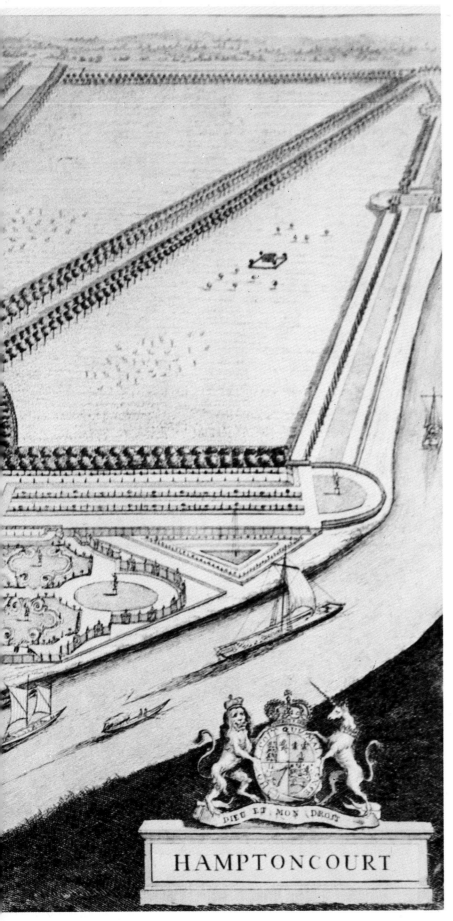

HAMPTONCOURT

Hampton Court after the Christopher Wren addition for William and Mary but before parterres were removed by Queen Anne (1702). Note patte d'oie (goosefoot) pattern of allées which are credited to one of the Mollets, brought from France to work in England by James I before 1625, nearly 40 years before Louis XIV began on Versailles. From I. Knyff, Britannia Illustrata, 1749.

Allée at Hampton Court, lined with beech trees.

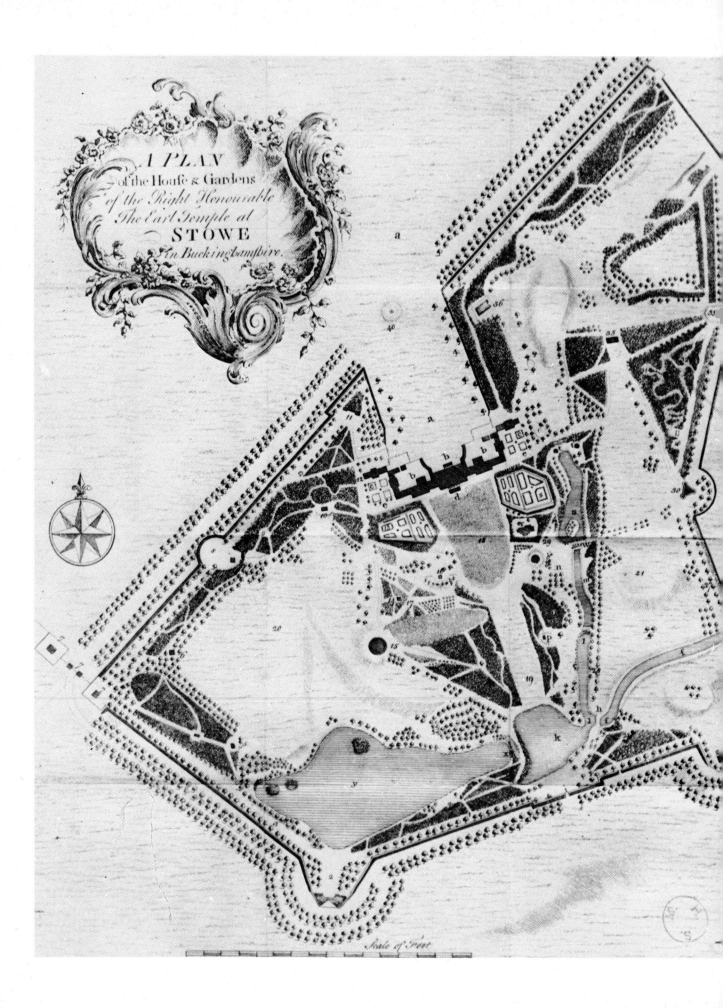

A PLAN
of the House & Gardens
of the Right Honourable
The Earl Temple at
STOWE
In Buckinghamshire.

Scale of Feet

Stowe is one of the most important gardens in England because it made the transition from the formal, geometric continental garden to the idealized natural English park of the 18th century. By 1790 Stowe was completed. Then, for more than a century, it was virtually abandoned, so it did not suffer the changes the 19th century wrought elsewhere. The famous Lancelot "Capability" Brown was undergardener at Stowe before going on to design the parklike estates throughout the British Isles that set the pattern for American public parks and estates. Plan from B. Seeley, Stowe, Buckingham, 1783.

the more original of the two. Where Le Nôtre was to express the ultimate in the geometric French garden, Brown a century later became the final, pure expression of the English park. After Le Nôtre came reaction, after Brown came disintegration.

When Lancelot Brown died in 1783 there was no single voice left to lead the gentry in a time when landscape as an art was as important as poetry and painting. Unfortunately, gardens are also subject to human action and reaction and are susceptible to fashion. Within five years a new leader appeared; his name was Humphry Repton.

Repton was not a creator. His role became more that of adapter, but fortunately he had respect for what Lancelot Brown had achieved before him. New plants had been pouring into England by the thousands and the cult of the collector was growing. As was to be expected, too, after living within the rigid limitations of a Brown park, another generation wanted change. Repton served this period well. He separated garden from park and theorized that if the park, in the tradition of Brown, should be natural then the garden should be natural and, likewise, if the garden were natural, the house should be, too. Obviously this was impossible, as a house can only be artificial (short of being a cave). Repton then carefully worked backward and successfully carried out the theory that the garden should contain some of the artificiality of the house and some of the naturalness of the park. His garden came, therefore, to serve as a transition between the two.

His most obvious device was to create a terrace close to the house, with a geometric arrangement of plants and garden spaces; yet at the edge of this terrace would be a balustrade so the park could be viewed beyond. Where it worked, it worked well, but soon the passion for hydrangeas and rhododendrons spilled over into the park itself, gradually cluttering and enclosing the broad vistas created by Lancelot Brown, which had been respected and, by and large, sensitively treated by Repton.

Lancelot Brown had interpreted beauty as gentleness, smoothness, grandeur. His critics argued for the picturesque, for a more rugged beauty. The difference was that between the gentle curve and sweep of the Thames, for instance, and the rough and more tortuous motion of a Scottish mountain stream. Where the Brown landscape contained nothing but gentle perfection, the picturesque school argued that rough rock outcroppings, jagged shorelines and storm-twisted trees were more "natural." Before they were through the followers of the picturesque erected dead tree trunks to satisfy their romantic painter's vision of landscape.

Once disintegration had set in, it could not be stopped. The idea of the picturesque was carried to such extremes that false ruins were constructed; falling aqueducts and crumbling bridges were built. Book upon book was published with plans showing how to disguise gate lodges, dairies, toolhouses and gardener's cottages to look like ruins of battlements or Gothic chapels. The collectors added their share to the dis-

Right: Palladian bridge, Stowe. Built in 1742, it is a copy of one built at Wilton five years earlier.

"Natural" lake was once an octagonal pool, sweep of lawn was formal terrace garden, Stowe. From Vergnaud, L'Art de Créer les Jardins, Paris, 1839.

integration process; the downfall of English gardens as fine art lay in the fact that plants from practically every corner of the earth grow beautifully in England.

As the botanical riches arrived, the exotic brilliance was impossible to ignore or confine to botanic collections. Landscapes had been a pastoral, quiet green. Houses were of somber color in order to blend with the park landscape. Interiors were wood-paneled, dull leather, muted tapestry, and the English sunshine is anything but generous. How, then, could an age so hungry for color possibly resist the flamboyant exotics? Soon the garden was no longer controlled by architects and poets and painters, but by plant experts and the horticulturally oriented professional gardeners as opposed to the landscape gardeners.

The idea that a garden should be a composition, a substantial work of art, died. It was a very quick death. Flower beds and one-of-a-kind shrubberies took over, and by the time the Victorians finished taste also seemed to be dead.

These new horticultural gardens also had great effect on America which, in the mid-19th century and even well into the 20th, seemed hopelessly ensnarled in copying mansions, public buildings and university halls from everywhere. For the horticulturally minded there was only one Mecca—England. English gardeners were imported by the boatload, and with them came the new English gardens, perennial borders, conservatories, "bedding out" and Victorian flamboyance.

Stowe, view from portico, Corinthian arch in distance, 1969.   121

"Capability" Brown created this lake at Blenheim Palace from small stream. It is often considered the "most perfect lake in England." "As we passed through the entrance archway and the lovely scenery burst upon me," wrote Lady Randolph Churchill on her first visit to Blenheim, "Randolph said with pardonable pride, 'This is the finest view in England.'"

Cattle Shed & Ruins

Plate 21.

A Termany in the Chinese Taste.

John Halfpenny Invt. delint.

After disintegration set in, English gardens
suffered romantic, fake ruins (above), Chinese
influence (right) and Victorian-collector. (opposite).
Illustrations from Taylor, Decorations for
Parks and Gardens, London, 1770; William Halfpenny,
Rural Architecture in the Chinese Taste (1755),
and portion of a garden illustration from
Brooke, The Gardens of England, London, 1857.

U.S.A.

Abby Aldrich Rockefeller Sculpture Garden, The Museum of Modern Art, New York City. Zion and Breen, Landscape Architects; photo by Alexandre Georges, The Museum of Modern Art.

Above: Central Park, in the heart of New York City and designed by Frederick Law Olmsted, English park landscape in concept. Photo by Alexander. Mount Vernon (colonnade left, p opposite) stems directly from the villas of ancient Rome and Renaissance in Italy becaus house, outbuildings and garden spaces are carefully organized to create a well-integrated unit. Photos courtesy Mount Vernon Ladies' Association. Above, right: This lovely shallow pool with its pebble mosaic gleaming through the water is at Dumbarton Oaks, Washington, D.C., and yet it speaks of ancestors in the Italian Renaissance. Photo Courtesy Dumbarton Oaks.

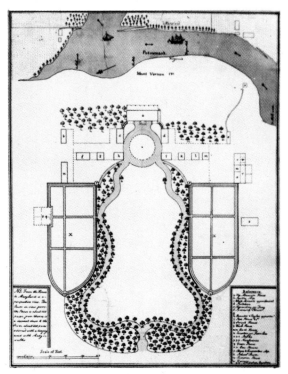

A New Beginning

America was wilderness. There were no cities, no monasteries, no villas or castles; there was no tradition of a people living for centuries in a place and evolving a way of building, of shaping, of *making* that place.

Although only a small part of the east coast of America was settled by Puritans, their stern code against beauty for its own sake, against art, had great impact on the rest of the country. Gardens for other than food and medicinal herbs were as intolerable to them as bright color, dancing and the celebration of Christmas. It was not a good beginning for the arts in America; Renaissance man was dead.

When a few important town-house gardens did appear in such places as Salem and Newburyport the patterns were geometric, based upon medieval prototypes. Utilitarian plants were dominant. Allées of pear trees, it appears, were more acceptable to the New England conscience than those of purely ornamental trees.

The more sophisticated gardens of Philadelphia and Williamsburg were frankly pleasure gardens, but their origin was William and Mary Dutch-English.

The suburb on the other hand was shaped by different factors. Open suburban yards stem directly from the fact that solid fences, hedges and dense shrub masses near houses were dangerous as long as marauding Indians were about. Open space meant protection, but the openness eventually came to be associated with democracy; so the neighbor who fenced himself in too securely became suspect. Zoning ordinances prohibit enclosing fences and hedges in much of suburbia even today, so hard do old attitudes die. Enclosure, or the lack thereof, also is a product of place. Where treeless prairies have become inhabited, it is more difficult to achieve enclosure than in areas that once were forest, where trees spring up naturally.

In the Southwest the missions shut out the sand and dangers of the desert by extending the building walls to enclose outdoor space, and in New Orleans the patio—deep, shaded and surrounded by the house—provided relief from a near-tropic sun. Turning inward, closing out the hostile elements of the outside world, both regions created well-defined garden spaces, but their roots were in Spain, North Africa and ancient Rome. Both seemed right for their place and time. But as the Conestoga wagons arrived, the attitudes of the east coast replaced the mission concept which otherwise might have become a dominant (and perhaps happy) basis for western gardens.

It was not until the dawn of the 20th century and the coming of Louis Sullivan that there arose a truly American expression for architecture; it came out of the Midwest. Almost half a century would pass before, out of the far West, a fresh idea was to arise for gardens.

When Thomas Church said that "gardens are for people," he expressed the new concept very well indeed. It was not really new. Romans, Moors and Renaissance men lounged, dined, played and made love in their gardens, but in America the idea of a garden as living space was new. And since

The new expression for gardens—truly American—started in California in the mid-20th century, with such men as Thomas Church, Garrett Eckbo and others. Photo of demonstration garden courtesy Los Angeles State and County Arboretum, Arcadia, California.

it was a place for people and for the objects that people use and enjoy, it depended upon the organization of these objects within the space through which people moved. Where earlier gardens had been dominated by architecture, paintings and images of "idealized" nature, these new gardens became sculptural in concept. "Being in a garden," said James Rose, "should be like being inside a piece of hollow sculpture."

California seemed to be the ideal place for the growth of this new garden. Domestic architecture and gardens changed rapidly until indoor and outdoor spaces became increasingly integrated. Living rooms flowed through glass walls to become living gardens, and the plants of the garden flowed back through the glass walls to create garden rooms. Materials such as wood, stone, concrete and steel were recognized and used honestly. Plants used individually or in carefully composed groups created a welcome relief from the frilly, plant-collector Victorians and self-conscious interior-decorator gardens that were too common.

These new gardens were indeed for people, and while for a long time they were referred to (not always kindly) as "California" gardens they were too good, too exciting and too much needed to be limited to California. Because these new gardens are more concerned with people than with patterns and plants they work well everywhere and allow a new freedom in recognizing and taking advantage of the site, be it Arizona desert or New Hampshire hillside.

Some of the most exciting of these new gardens are public, or at least for public use. Mellon Square, Hartford's Constitution Plaza and new parks, squares, plazas and malls are providing comfortable, enjoyable oases for people in cities large and small across the land. They are truly gardens for people. And while in the past the history of gardens has been told in terms of emperors and cardinals and landed gentry, it may be that in America new garden history is being made in terms more democratic, and "the greater perfection" is, at long last, being achieved.

Left: Many of the new American gardens are for public or semipublic use. The park of the Connecticut General Life Insurance Company, Bloomfield, Connecticut, has Noguchi sculpture, native trees in a rolling terrain. Architects Skidmore, Owens and Merrill; photo Ezra Stoller, courtesy Connecticut General Life Insurance Company. Below: Mellon Square, a park over a garage, is an exciting place for people in downtown Pittsburgh. Design by Simonds and Simonds; photo J. W. Molitor.

Waterfall, Lovejoy Plaza, Portland, Oregon, provides excitement for children, relief from heat. Design by Lawrence Halprin & Associates; photo Maude Dorr.

Vaux-le-Vicomte.

II. A GARDEN IS AN EXPERIENCE

A garden is an experience.

James C. Rose
CREATIVE GARDENS

No occupation is so delightful to me as
the culture of the earth, and no culture
comparable to that of the garden.
I am still devoted to the garden. But
though an old man, I am but a
young gardener.

Thomas Jefferson

Preceding pages: Allée of lindens at Champs,
near Paris. Opposite: Live oaks with Spanish
moss, Middleton Place, near Charleston, South
Carolina. Above: Azalea, Magnolia Gardens,
near Charleston. Succeeding pages: Artichoke
farm, Carmel, California.

Preceding pages: Bridge at Blenheim. Opposite: Elizabethan garden, Hampton Court. Above: Lily-flowering tulips. Left: Tjou gate at entrance to grass allée, Hampton Court (see plan view, pages 112-113).

Villa Lante, lower parterre (see plan, pages 76-77).

Fountain of the Giants and banquet table with wine-cooling trough,
Villa Lante. Right: Fountain of the Moors, Villa Lante. Succeeding pages: Azalea hedge, Columbia, South Carolina.

Wall of One Hundred Fountains, Villa d'Este (see plan, page 83).

Left to right: Villa d'Este, Fountain of the Dragons; Stair of the Boiling Sound; Round Place of the Cypresses. Allée, Versailles.

156　　*Alhambra, Court of the Lions.*

Alhambra, climbing roses.

God Almighty esteemed the life of a man in a garden the happiest He could give him, or else He would not have placed Adam in that of Eden. . . . As gardening has been the inclination of Kings and the choice of Philosophers so it has been the common favourite of public and private men: a pleasure of the greatest, and a care of the meanest; and, indeed, an employment and possession for which no man is too high or too low.

Sir William Temple
OF THE GARDENS OF
EPICURUS (1685)

The architect and the gardener do not understand each other, and commonly the owner or resident is totally at variance in his tastes and intentions from both; or the man whose ideas the plan is made to serve, or who pays for it, has no true independent taste, but had fancies to be accommodated, which only follow confusedly after custom or fashion. I think, with Ruskin, it is a pity that every man's house cannot be really his own, and that he cannot make all that is true, beautiful, and good in his own character, tastes, pursuits, and history manifest in it.

Frederick Law Olmsted
WALKS AND TALKS OF AN
AMERICAN FARMER IN ENGLAND

Preceding pages: Iceland poppies, Pasadena, California. Above: Cherokee rose and wisteria, Charleston, South Carolina. Opposite: Canephorae at edge of Canopus, Hadrian's villa.

. . . the name given to a thing is not
the subject, it is only a convenient label.
The subject is inexhaustible.

George Bellows

Preceding pages: Colonnade of the Canopus.
Above: Waterlilies, Claude Monet; canvas
$35^{1}/_{4}$ x $39^{1}/_{4}$ *inches; signed and dated 1905.*
Gift of Edward Jackson Holmes, Museum of Fine
Arts, Boston. Opposite: Waterlilies,
Dover, Massachusetts.

Opposite: Lampranthus, Los Angeles City and County Arboretum, Arcadia. Above, left: Horse-chestnut, Alexandria, Virginia. Below: Hosta, buttercups and Johnny jump-ups. Right: Saucer magnolia, Swarthmore, Pennsylvania.

167

Corn and cockscomb six-fold Japanese screen. Attributed to Nonomura Sotatsu (early 17th century). Kate S. Buckingham Collection; courtesy The Art Institute of Chicago.

170   *Red-twigged dogwood, Arnold Arboretum, Boston.*

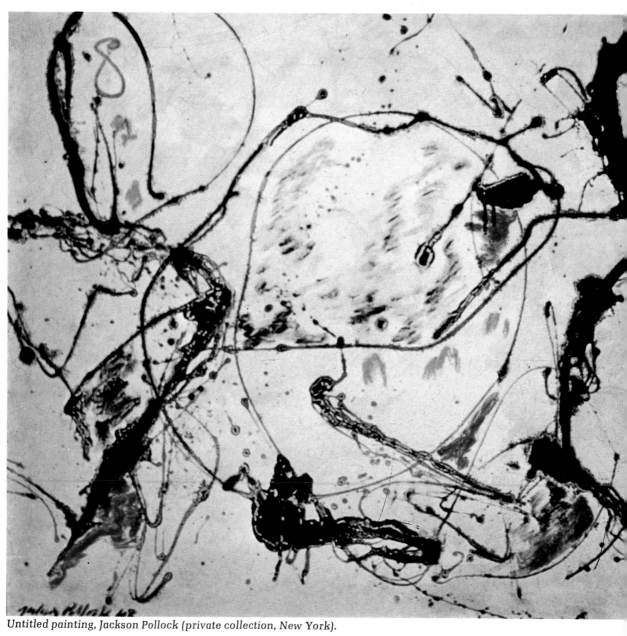

Untitled painting, Jackson Pollock (private collection, New York).

Blueberry in autumn, Topsfield, Massachusetts.

They are fools who call my work
abstract. What they think to be abstract
is the most realistic, because what is
real is not the outer form but the idea,
the essence of things.

Constantin Brancusi

Monterey cypress on rocks, Point Lobos, California.

It would be dangerous indeed to suggest that Jackson Pollock was painting the blueberry bush (on page 173), or that Afro was painting the Queen Anne's lace and black-eyed Susans (opposite). And yet, were they not painting them even while not painting them? Or is it coincidence that the paintings and photographs resemble each other?

Plato is reported to have said something to the effect that the truth of the tree is in the treeness of the tree. If we consider all the trees we know—elm, oak, short, tall, squat, slender, craggy, graceful, young, old, leafy and winter-nude—we immediately see that even so astoundingly simple a word as *tree* is not easy to define. And since Plato equated truth with reality and defined it as "that which is," he argued that the physical tree—bark, wood, bud, flower, fruit—was quite fleeting and therefore not real. The physical tree became secondary to the tree as a concept; the tree as an idea became reality.

And since a concept is of necessity an abstraction, Plato's example suggests that the abstraction is real, and what we usually take for granted as being real is not real at all:

It has always been my desire to take down from the wall any one of a number of large Jackson Pollock paintings and shape it into a cylinder—or, better still, a sphere—and get inside. If Pollock was not painting the forest from which we sprang he was without doubt concerned with it. It may have been only one of many things he was trying to say about the world in which we live: state-

Sunflower, Wayne, Pennsylvania.

ments distilled so that we may grasp a fresh view but, if we are lucky, on our own terms and according to our own experience.

The danger of exposing ourselves to any art—including gardens—is that we see only details, limit ourselves to labels and fail to comprehend the sum and substance of what the artist has said.

Gardens, like paintings and symphonies, are beyond words.

Queen Anne's lace with black-eyed Susans, Valley Forge, Pennsylvania.

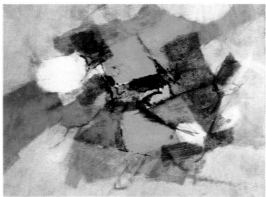

"Night Flight," Afro, 1957, oil on canvas,
$44^7/_8$ x $57^3/_8$ inches, The Solomon R. Guggenheim
Museum, New York.

Tree peony, Beverly, Massachusetts.

Even the general
    Took off his armor
    To gaze
At our peonies

        Kikaku (1661-1707)
        HAIKU HARVEST

Squash blossom, South Hamilton, Massachusetts.

Garden with birches, West Campton, New Hampshire.

AFTER THE THUNDER

The storm has left the air in a fluster.
Things come to life, draw breath, like Eden.
Spreading a purple-handed cluster
The lilac scoops a stream of freshness.

Things come to life with the shift of weather.
The drainpipe overflows with showers.
Behind black cloud a light sky towers
In range on range of blue on blue.

More vigorous even than the weather
To wash the world, the artist's hand
Dips life in dyes and issues brand
New legends and realities.

Now fifty years of memory
Recede with the receding storm.
Time to accept another stage;
The century has come of age.

It's not the earthquake that controls
The advent of a different life,
But storms of generosity
And visions of incandescent souls.

Boris Pasternak
POEMS 1955-1959

Seed pods bursting, milkweed, Valley Forge, Pennsylvania.

IV. THE IN-LISTENING EAR

Theophrastus: The Father of Botany

A voiceless flower
   Speaks
     To the obedient
In-listening ear
       Onitsura
       HAIKU HARVEST

Of all of the men who ever lived upon the earth certainly one of the most remarkable was Theophrastus of Eresus who was born about 370 B.C. on the isle of Lesbos (modern Mytilene) in the Aegean Sea and is regarded as the Father of Botany. Incredibly enough, only about one-twentieth of his voluminous writings were about botany, but his *Historia Plantarum* is the foundation of all we know about plants today.

Born into an already sophisticated environment in the city of Eresus, Theophrastus became a student of Plato at an early age. Plato died when Theophrastus was 22; after that he became a student and later a close friend and fellow teacher of Aristotle. When Aristotle died he bequeathed his manuscripts, books and botanic garden to Theophrastus who was then 48 years old. Because of his involvement with a school of some 2,000 students and his investigations into many other matters, Theophrastus had little time for travel; so the botanic garden willed to him by Aristotle along with the manuscripts must have been the chief source of information and observation for his botanical writings.

Some historians give Aristotle credit for the origin of botany. In fact the term "Aristotelian botany" is sometimes used, but it was Theophrastus who organized and recorded this basic plant information. No doubt his long association with Aristotle had a profound influence on him and the investigations and deepest thinking of the two men came together. From this beginning has grown the structure of our plant knowledge.

In the page reproduced opposite (from a 1495/98 edition in Greek of his *Historia Plantarum*) Theophrastus discusses the problem of what should be considered plant parts and how to label them. Is bark, for instance, a part, or is it but a submaterial of the stem (and even then only certain stems) which should be considered the part? As a result of careful thought, he designated the basic parts: root, stem, leaf, flower, fruit.

Theophrastus also separated woody plants from herbaceous plants and subdivided these two groups into (for the first) trees and shrubs and (for the second) perennials, biennials and annuals. At the same time he was careful to point out that some trees could sometimes appear shrublike and that a shrub could look like a tree depending upon culture and/or growing conditions.

Even more difficult was separating the animal kingdom from the plant kingdom and deciding what to include in the latter. Theophrastus admitted that it was very difficult but stated that "plants are not, like animals, endowed with ethical susceptibilities and the power of voluntary action." Theophrastus also made it clear that fungi, lichens, algae and seaweed were to be included in the plant kingdom.

"I bequeath to my friends," he wrote, "who are especially named in this my Will, and those that will spend their time with them in learning and philosophy, my garden, walk and houses adjoining; upon certain conditions however that none of them shall claim any particular property therein, or alienate them from their proper use, but

ΘΕΟΦΡΑΣΤΟΥ ΠΕΡΙ ΦΥΤΩΝ ΙΣΤΟΡΙΑΣ ΤΟ ·Α

Pyrus.

Pears, from Theophrastus, De Historia Plantarum, Amsterdam, 1644.

Opening page of a Greek edition of Theophrastus, published in Venice, 1495-1498.

that they shall be enjoyed in common by them all, as a sacred place where they may familiarly visit one another and discourse together like good friends."

Theophrastus' *Historia Plantarum* survived the centuries from his death until the invention of printing in the mid-15th century. It was among the first books to be printed and, as if reborn, it began to appear again and again, in Greek, in Latin, in German, in English, until by 1866 more than 20 editions had appeared in practically every European language. It was quoted and referred to over and over again in herbals of the 15th and 16th centuries and came to be considered the standard botanical text.

The Herbalists

"To make folk mery at ye table," advises the *Grete Herball* (1526), "take foure leves and foure rotes of vervain [verbena] in wyne, then spryncle the wyne all about the house where the eatynge is and they shall be all mery."

Melancholia appears to have been a common malady of the time because prescriptions for its cure are frequent in the herbals (medical handbooks) of the 15th, 16th and 17th centuries. Medicine depended upon plants for its remedies, so herbals, amusing though they may appear today, really concerned themselves with more serious conditions of human health or the lack thereof.

From the time of the invention of printing until the early 20th century hundreds of herbals were printed, but as botany and medicine grew apart the herbal disappeared. Its medical information became a part of the strictly medical *pharmacopoeia* and the botanical information evolved into the *florae.*

The *Grete Herball* is not one of the most important of herbals, but it was the first to be printed in English. It is a translation of an earlier French herbal, *Le Grand Herbier,* which itself is of misty origin. Yet the *Grete Herball* was a practical handbook giving "... parfyt knowledge and understanding of all manner of herbes and there gracyous vertues...."

The title "German Fathers of Botany" is applied to a group of herbalists of the first half of the 16th century. Otto Brunfels published *Herbarum vive eicones* in Strassburg in 1530. Because the illustrations represent plants as they appear rather than in the styl-ized manner of earlier herbals, Brunfels' herbal is considered a definite step forward. His text, however, is largely borrowed from earlier writers.

Another member of the German group, a contemporary of Brunfels, was Hieronymus Bock. His work is not noted for its illustrations but rather for its descriptions of plants. He was a keen collector and described only plants that he personally observed and thereby set the pattern for future *florae.*

The greatest of the German Fathers of Botany was Leonhart Fuchs (1501-1566); his *De historia stirpium,* published in 1542, has been called the most beautiful of all herbals. In his herbal, Leonhart Fuchs lists about 400 native German plants and about 100 foreign ones, including the first published illustrations and descriptions of some American plants such as Indian corn and pumpkin.

The scholarship and integrity of Leonhart Fuchs and his impatience with the lack of it are revealed in his introduction: "...but by Immortal God, is it to be wondered at that kings and princes do not at all regard the pursuit of the investigation of plants, when even physicians of our time so shrink from it that it is scarcely possible to find one among a hundred who has an accurate knowledge of even so many as a few plants? ...And so it comes to pass that the druggists —God knows that they themselves are for the most part an illiterate set—leave all this to foolish and superstitious old women who gather herbs and roots. Error is therefore

Herb gatherers, The Grete Herball, London, 1526.

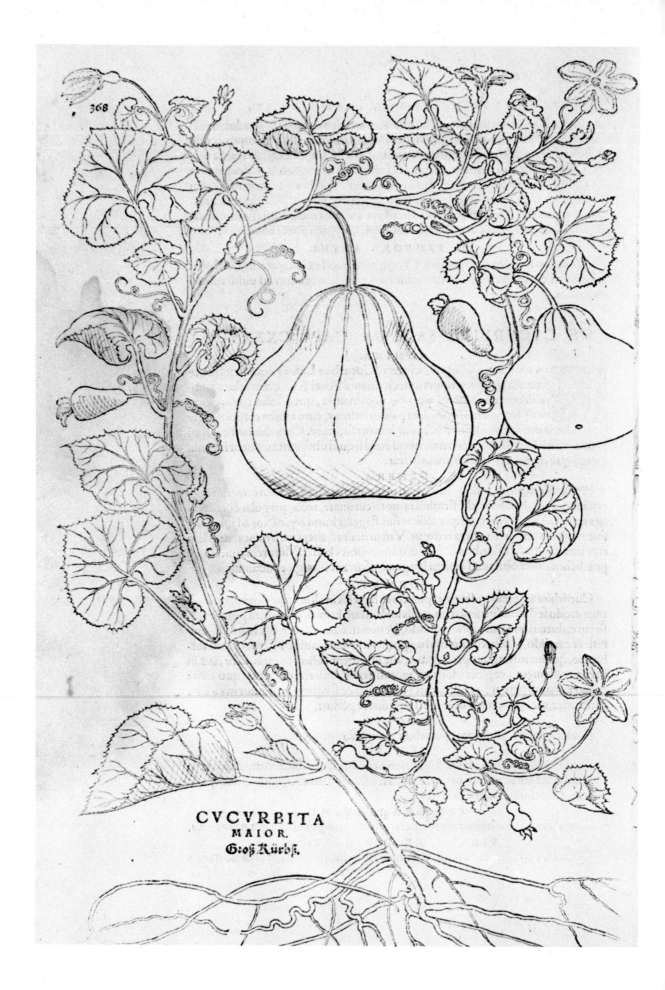

CVCVRBITA
MAIOR.
Groß Kürbß.

heaped on error, and will be so long as the identification of vegetable medicines is left to rustic and vulgar ignorance."

Perhaps to emphasize that the Germans did not have a corner on the market for botanists, William Turner, physician and divine, was dubbed "Father of British Botany." As did many of his German counterparts, he, too, became involved with the Reformation, and a ban was placed on his writings during the reign of Henry VIII. Turner also spent some time in prison, and the Bishop of Bath wrote of "...his undiscrete behavior in the pulpitt: where he medleth with all matters...." William Turner's important work, his *Herbal*, was published in three installments, from 1551 to 1562.

Turner took great pride in having observed the herbs he described and often traveled great distances to do so: "...I wente into Italye and into diverse partes of Germany to knowe and se the herbes my selfe."

Many superstitions surrounded the gathering and use of herbs. One of the most persistent had to do with a plant called mandrake which was popularly endowed with supernatural powers. The root of this plant was thought to appear in human form. Turner was not the first to discredit the legend of the mandrake but he also points out, "The rootes which are conterfited and made like litle puppettes and mamettes...are nothyng elles but folishe feined trifles,...so trymmed of crafty theves to mocke the poore people with all, and to rob them both of theyr wit and theyr money."

Of all the English herbals none is better known than that of John Gerard, "Master in Chirurgerie," and extremely capable gardener. He owned and maintained a famous garden in the then fashionable Holborn section of London and maintained other gardens for Lord Burleigh. His massive *The Herball or General Historie of Plantes,* which was published by John Norton in 1597, contains over 1,800 woodcuts, among which is the first known illustration of the Virginia potato. When anyone thinks of herbals in the English language, it is this one that comes to mind first—yet it is nearly a total fraud.

John Norton, the publisher, had commissioned a Dr. Priest to translate the final work of Rembert Dodoens (or Dodonaeus), the Belgian herbalist, which was published in 1583. Dr. Priest died before the work was completed, so Gerard took over the translation, completed it, rearranged it and published it as his own. His colossal nerve extended so far as to write, in his address to the reader in the front of the herbal, that he had heard that there was a Dr. Priest who had started a translation of Dodoens but, "being prevented by death, his translation likewise perished."

The final and most unbelievable twist to this tale comes in an endorsing letter at the start of the herbal from a Stephen Bredwell, which contradicts Gerard's statement in his own book! "D. Priest," wrote Bredwell, "for his translation of so much as Dodonaeus, hath hereby left a tombe for his honorable sepulture. Master Gerard comming last, but not the least, hath many waies accommo-

The woodblocks of Fuchs' De historia stirpium, 1542, published in Basel, Switzerland, are considered a landmark in the history of plant illustration. Shown here is a pumpkin from the New World.

dated the...worke unto our English nation."

Of the woodcuts, only about one percent are original, the remainder are from a work by Tabernaemontanus (1590), which John Norton had obtained from Frankfurt. Gerard's botanical knowledge was so slender that he could not match the woodblocks with the plant descriptions and Norton called in an expert to help, but Gerard's impatience soon ended this collaboration and the herbal first appeared with many errors.

In spite of the manner in which Gerard's herbal came into being, his attempt to simplify the language, and Norton's clear Roman typefaces, helped create a place for it, and the herbal was in fact revised by Thomas Johnson, amended and corrected and republished in 1633 and again in 1636.

This *Colutea* or bastard Sene, doth differ from that plant κολυτεα with υ in the second syllable, of which *Colytea Theophrastus* writeth in his thirde booke.

* The temperature and vertues.

Theophrastus, neither any other of the ancients haue made mention of the temperature or facul- A ties in working of these plants, more then that it is good to fatten cattle, especially sheepe, as the same authour affirmeth.

Of Licorice.   Chap. 10.

1 *Glycyrrhiza Echinata Dioscoridis.*
Hedgehogge Licorice.

2 *Glycyrriza vulgaris.*
Common Licorice.

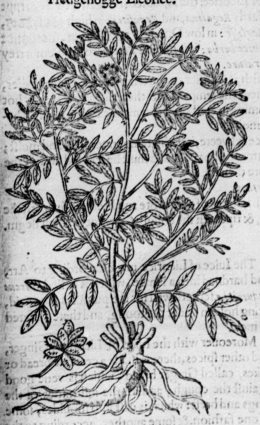

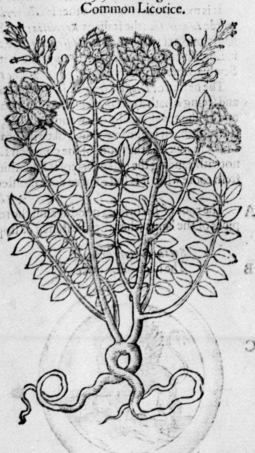

* The description.

1   THe first kinde of Licorice hath many woodie branches, rising vp to the height of two or three cubits, beset with leaues of an ouerworne greene colour, consisting of many small leaues set vpon a middle rib, like the leaues of *Colutea*, or the Mastich tree, somewhat gluti- nous in handling: among which come small knops growing vpon short stems betwixt the leaues and the branches, clustering togither and making a round forme or shape: out of which grow small blew flowers, of the colour of the English Hyacinth; after which succeede rounde, rough, prickley heads, consisting of diuers rough or scalie husks closely and thicke compact togither; in which is conteined a flat seede: the roote is straight, yellow within, and browne without; of a sweete and pleasant taste.

2   The common and vsuall Licorice, hath stalkes and leaues very like the former, sauing that his leaues are greener and greater, and the flowers of a shining blew colour; but the flowers and cods grow not so thicke clustring togither in round heads as the former, but spike fashion, or rather like

the wilde Vetch called *Onobrychis*, or *Galega* : the cods are small and flat like vnto the Tare : the rootes are of a brownish colour without, and yellow within like Boxe, and sweeter in taste then the former.

❋ The place.

These plants do grow in sundry places of Germanie wilde, and in Fraunce and Spaine, but they are planted in gardens in England, whereof I haue plentie in my garden : the poore people of the north parts of England do manure it with great diligence, whereby they obtaine great plenty therof, replanting the same once in three or fower yeeres.

❋ The time.

Licorice flowreth in Iuly, and the seede is ripe in September.

❋ The names.

The first is called in Greek γλυκύῤῥιζα: in Latine *Dulcis radix*, or sweete Roote : this Licorice is not knowne either to the Apothecaries or to the vulgar people; we call it in English *Diosc*. his Licorice.

It is most euident that the other is *Glycyrrhiza*, or Licorice : the Apothecaries call it by a corrupt worde *Liquiritia* : the Italians *Regolitia* : the Spaniards *Regaliza*, and *Regalitia* : in high Suszhotz, Suszwurtzel : in French *Rigolisse, Raigalisse*, and *Reglisse* : in low Dutch Calissiehout, suethout : in English common Licorice : *Pliny* calleth it *Scythica herba* : it is named *Scythice* of the countrey Scythia, where it groweth.

❋ The temperature.

The nature of *Dioscorides* his Licorice as *Galen* saith, is familiar to the temperature of our bodies, and seeing it hath a certaine binding qualitie adioined, the temperature thereof so much as is hot and binding, is especially of a warme qualitie, comming neerest of all to a meane temperature ; besides, for that it is also sweete, it is likewise meanely moist.

For as much as the roote of the common Licorice is sweete, it is also temperately hot and moist ; notwithstanding the barke thereof is something bitter and hot, but this must be scraped away ; the fresh roote when it is full of iuice doth moisten more then the dry.

❋ The vertues.

A   The root of Licorice is good against the rough harshnes of the throte and brest ; it openeth the pipes of the lungs when they be stuffed or stopped, & ripeneth the cough, & bringeth forth flegm.

B
Succus Glycyrrhiza.
The iuice of Licorice.

C

D

E

F

G

H

The Iuice of Licorice made according to Art, and hardned into a lumpe, which is called *Succus Liquiritia*, serueth well for the purposes aforesaid, being holden vnder the toong, and there suffered to melt.

Moreouer with the Iuice of Licorice, Ginger, and other spices, there is made a certaine bread or cakes, called Ginger bread, which is verie good against the cough, and all the infirmities of the lungs and brest : which is cast into mouldes, some of one fashion, & some another, according to the fancie of the Apothecaries, as the pictures set foorth do shew for example.

The Iuice of Licorice is profitable against the heate of the stomacke, and of the mouth.   I

The same is drunk with wine of Raisons against the infirmities of the liuer and chest, scabs or sores of the bladder, and diseases of the kidneies.

Being melted vnder the toong it quencheth thirst ; it is good for greene woundes being laide thereupon, and for the stomacke if it be chewed.

The decoction of the fresh rootes serueth for the same purposes.

But the dry roote most finely powdred, is a singular good remedy for a pin and a web of the eie, if it be strowed thereupon.

Dioscorides

  Rounds are cough-drop "cakes" (from Gerard's Herball, London, 1597)

Paradise in the Sun

John Parkinson, apothecary to James I and Charles I, was an herbalist and, like John Gerard, Thomas Johnson and John Tradescant, created one of the famous London gardens of his time. He did publish an herbal, *Theatrum botanicum: The Theater of Plants, Or, An Herball of a Large Extent* . . . in 1640, but for horticulturists his most interesting work is *Paradisi in Sole Paradisus Terrestris*, published in 1629. It would be difficult not to admire the wit and audacity of a man who would pun on his own name in his title: "earthly paradise of park-in-sun."

Mr. Parkinson, however, gave his age much practical information; his garden information is of the down-to-earth, feet-on-the-ground variety:

"Because that Carnations and Gilloflowers [clove pinks] bee the chiefest flowers of account in all our English Gardens, I have thought good to entreate somewhat amply of them. . . ." He devotes five large pages of instructions to the cultivation of carnations and pinks in the beginning of his book and ten more pages plus three plates to listing and describing the kinds later on. His instructions are practical, his attitude admirable: "The way to encrease Gilloflowers by slipping, is so common with all that ever kept any of them, that I think most persons may thinke me idle, to spend time to set downe in writing that which is so well known unto all. . . . For I am assured, the greatest number doe use, and follow the most usuall way, and that is not alwaies the best, especially when by good experience a better way is found, and may be learned;

and therefore if some can doe a thing better than others, I thinke it is no shame to learne it of them."

According to Parkinson, an emerging tulip ". . . springeth out of the ground with his leaves folded one within another, the first or lowest leafe riseth up first, sharp pointed, and folded round together, untill it be an inch or two above the ground, which then openeth it selfe, shewing another leafe folded also in the . . . belly of the first. . . ."

The heads of "Sunne Flower," he comments, "are dressed, and eaten as Hartichokes are . . . but they are too strong for my taste." And of marigolds he points out that they have no "Vertues" (practical use), ". . . but are cherished in Gardens for their beautifull flowers sake."

Primroses, on the other hand, seem to have special value for easing "paines in the head" and also for ". . . the Palsie, and paines of the joynts . . . which hath caused the names of *Arthritica*, *Paralysis*, and *Paralytica*, to bee given them." Let us be thankful that these names did not stick to the lovely genus *Primula*.

In spite of Parkinson's somewhat pompous opening sermon on Eden, it is impossible not to respond to his writing and to visualize him as anything but a warm and friendly plantsman eager to share his experience. At the close of his thorough chapter on the culture of carnations he states, ". . . if anyone have any other better way, I shall be as willing to learne it of them, as I have beene to give them or any others the knowledge of that I have here set downe."

The Adventurous Physician

Intellectual curiosity, fearlessness, knowledge, wanderlust and youth: this was the German physician Engelbert Kaempfer, who was born in Westphalia in 1651. He was the son of a pastor and attended several schools before receiving his Ph.D. at Cracow. Later he studied medicine and natural sciences in Prussia. Before he was 30, Kaempfer had established himself at Uppsala, in Sweden, where many urged him to remain, but his taste for adventure was too strong. In 1683 he joined a Swedish mission to Russia and Persia and the following year reached Isfahan, the Persian capital.

After four years in Persia, Kaempfer was appointed chief surgeon to the fleet of the Dutch East India Company in the Persian Gulf, and in June 1688 he set sail for Java, Ceylon, Bengal and Batavia, which he reached in the fall of 1689. The following spring he sailed for Japan where the Company maintained an outpost at Nagasaki.

The Japanese were suspicious of outsiders, so the representatives of the Dutch East India Company were not permitted ashore and were confined to a small, stockaded, artificial island in the harbor. Fortunately the custom of the time required the nobility and officials to make an annual pilgrimage to the court of the Shogun in Tokyo (then Yeddo) and Kaempfer accompanied the Dutch ambassador on this trip in 1691 and again in 1692. On both occasions the trip took approximately two months (from March to May). For Kaempfer, of course, they were wonderful opportunities to observe the flora of the countryside, the people and the towns and cities along the way. But he was much more enterprising than to allow himself these opportunities alone. Even on his stockaded island he managed to gain the confidence of the Japanese and got them to bring him many plant specimens.

His limitations of observing plants in the field are indicated by his illustrations of lilies that are short-stemmed and therefore must have been drawn from cut specimens. Among those he recorded is the Tiger lily (*L. tigrinum*) which is so common to gardens in New England and to the West, where it was carried in covered wagons along with day lilies and lilacs, that it is often taken to be a native plant. Kaempfer also saw the

Ginkgo (above), camellia and tea (opposite), all three illustrated by Engelbert Kaempfer in his Amoenitatum Exoticarum, *1712.*

lovely reflexed Speciosum lily (*L. speciosum*), the pink version of which is commonly called Rubrum lily. He described it: ". . . a flower of magnificent beauty, shiny white with a pink flush, warty with glistening blood red spots, the petals curved back into a globe. . . ." When Linnaeus wrote the first edition of *Species Plantarum* in 1753, which was the start of modern plant nomenclature, his knowledge of plants of Japan was limited to what he learned from studying Kaempfer.

The only work by Kaempfer published during his lifetime is *Amoenitatum Exoticarum Politico-Physico-Medicarum*, in 1712. It is a remarkable story of his journeys and observations, but an even greater storehouse of his writings and drawings is now in the British Museum.

Physician, naturalist, botanist, illustrator of no small talent and author of the remarkable *Amoenitatum Exoticarum*, Kaempfer was not only the pioneer investigator of Persian flora and the first to record Japanese plants accurately, but his contributions to yet another field—history—were equally remarkable. His *History of Japan* was translated and published in English in 1727 in London. For more than a century it served as the most authoritative reference work on late 17th-century Japan and remains today an important historical document.

Linnaeus: The Great Swede

"It was a splendid spring day; the sky was clear and warm, while the west wind refreshed one with a delicious breath. The winter rye stood six inches high and the barley had newly come into leaf. The birch was beginning to shoot, and all trees were leafing, except the elm and aspen. Though only few of the spring flowers were in bloom, it was obvious that the whole land was smiling with the coming of spring."

So, in 1732, Linnaeus recorded the day on which he set out from Uppsala upon his five-month exploration of Lapland. He was 25 years old, a student of medicine and an inspired naturalist with a sharp eye and a quick mind. Lapland was then a dark mystery which had been but little explored.

As a student at Uppsala, Linnaeus studied under and lived in the home of J. O. Rudbeck, professor of botany. Rudbeck had visited Lapland in 1695, but his collections of plant, animal and bird specimens had been destroyed in a fire in 1702 before they could be recorded and the results published. Linnaeus no doubt was sympathetic to the great loss suffered by his teacher, but he also could hardly resist the lure of the northland. It was a dangerous, extremely difficult and in many ways dreadful trip. While he had already gained respect for many for his unusual abilities, the Lapland trip projected Linnaeus into new prominence. Later, when he traveled to Holland to obtain his medical degree, Linnaeus found that he was already

Venus fly trap, sent to Linnaeus from the Carolinas. Illustration from John Ellis, Directions for Bringing Over Seeds and Plants From the East Indies, London, 1770.

known for his expedition as well as for the new and startling ideas he had put forth at Uppsala.

The breadth of Linnaeus' interests is revealed in a letter written by a friend, J. Browallius, shortly after the Lapland adventure. "You should have seen his museum, which was available for his audience, it would have struck you with surprise and delight. The ceiling he had adorned with birds' skins, one wall with a Lapp costume and other curiosities, while a second boasted medical books, with physical and chemical instruments and stones. The upper part of a corner was occupied with tree-branches, with thirty different kinds of tame fowl, and in the window stood big pots of rare plants. Besides, one had the opportunity of seeing his collection of dried plants pasted on paper, all collected in Sweden, and amounting to more than three thousand kinds, wild or cultivated, to which must be added the Lapland rarest plants also dried and pressed. Furthermore were a thousand species of insects, and about as many of Swedish minerals, placed on wide shelves and in the most pleasing way arranged after Linnaeus's own system, founded in accordance with his observations."

Linnaeus applied his mind to the then confused world of botany in order to establish a logical system for naming plants. Before him, plant names were in confusion; herbals of the 15th, 16th and 17th centuries were full of complex polynomials—long plant names made up of a series of descriptive words. In Switzerland a botanist named Gaspard Bauhin had published descriptions of some 6,000 plants in 1623. In naming these plants he used a two-word (binomial) system and urged its adoption, but progress sometimes cometh slow. It was nearly a century later that Linnaeus was able to accomplish what Bauhin had started.

The basis of the binomial system requires all plants to be grouped according to genera. Each genus is subdivided into species. Roses belong to the genus *Rosa* and pines to the genus *Pinus*. The common pasture rose of the eastern United States is *Rosa virginiana,* the Rugose rose of the seaside is *Rosa rugosa.* Eastern white pine is *Pinus strobus,* pitch pine *Pinus rigida* and Scots pine *Pinus sylvestris.* The beauty of such a system is that it can be expanded endlessly; new species can be added to each genus without limit. Many plants of the world are yet to be discovered, so the need for an expandable system, two centuries after Linnaeus, is still with us.

Linnaeus brought the binomial system into being and almost universal acceptance with the publication of his *Species Plantarum* in 1753. In it he described the known species of the time, about 8,000 plants. In his new descriptions he separated the essential from the nonessential and added critical differentiating remarks on the old names. This is the foundation upon which present-day plant nomenclature is built.

It is necessary in any science to be able to communicate across language and international barriers. The *International Code of Botanical Nomenclature* accepts and establishes Linnaeus as the beginning. When the letter L. appears after a botanical name, such as for white pine *(Pinus strobus L.),* it means that the plant was given that name by Linnaeus. Although the name might have been modified by him to fit into the binomial system, he is nevertheless credited as the author of the name. Plants discovered, named and recorded since Linnaeus are also credited with authorship so researchers can rely on the origin of every plant name.

The international rules also provide for the handling of a given name when applied to two plants and to the problem of one plant with two names. While to the amateur the intricacies of plant names can be confusing, the system is exceptionally well organized and the regularly held international congresses for botany and horticulture have become forums of remarkable agreement and achievement.

Even if Linnaeus had worked only in the field of botany, his name would stand forever as one of the great scientific minds of all time. Certainly he was Sweden's brightest son, and we still benefit from him. As a doctor he attacked dietary prejudices and classified certain fevers in terms of origin. He was sure that many diseases were caused by "living particles" (bacteria) and wrote and lectured extensively on public health and unnecessary bleeding (a much-practiced remedy at the time), and his *Materia medica* became a classic in pharmacological literature.

To the science of geology he added knowledge on the origin of crystals and their ap-plication to the classification of minerals. For zoology he applied the principles of botanical nomenclature and introduced a definite terminology. He also determined that whales were mammals and not fish. He had hundreds of students and dozens of disciples who combed the world for plant specimens that were sent back to Uppsala for identification, naming and recording. His herbarium specimens—an extremely important reference for botanists for 200 years —are now in London, the property of the Linnean Society of London.

"With clear-sightedness, without fear, but without arrogance," wrote T. M. Fries (translated by Benjamin Jackson, 1923), one of Linnaeus' important biographers, "he undertook to elucidate all questions which previous botanists had put forward, and thus he effected a revolution. Botanic language he sorted out from its barbaric confusion, giving the requisite precision to each botanic concept; for descriptive purposes he decided and settled simple and still valid laws. . . . Briefly, in small things and great, he showed himself an unsurpassed master in bringing order, light and system where ignorance and indifference had produced obscurity and confusion."

In addition to it all, the beloved "Great Swede" was also a superior teacher who opened doors to new horizons for the many who came after him. "A professor," he said, "can never better distinguish himself in his work than by encouraging a clever pupil, for the true discoverers are amongst them, as comets amongst the stars."

John Bartram: Ploughman to Botanist

"One day I was very busy in holding my plough (for thee seest I am but a ploughman) and being weary, I ran under the shade of a tree to repose myself. I cast my eyes on a daisy, I plucked it mechanically, and viewed it with more curiosity than common country farmers are wont to do. . . ."

These words, quoted in a letter of a visiting gentleman in 1769, catch the spirit of John Bartram who, when he was about 30 years old, decided to devote his life to increasing his knowledge of the natural world. His botanical beginning was a Latin grammar purchased in Philadelphia. With the help of a neighboring schoolmaster he was able to read Linnaeus at the end of three months. From his farm his explorations spread until, before his death in 1777 at the age of 78, he had explored the Susquehanna and Allegheny rivers as well as Lake Ontario and Lake George in the North. He also traveled southward to the Carolinas, Georgia and Florida as Botanist to the King (George III).

Soon after Bartram's explorations began, a Philadelphia merchant established a connection between Bartram and Peter Collinson, a London wool merchant, who was much interested in plants. Collinson in many ways was responsible for the scope of Bartram's contributions because of his contacts with English and European botanists and other plantsmen.

For nearly 35 years, plants and seeds flowed from Bartram through Collinson to Linnaeus, Mark Catesby, John Fothergill, Philip Miller, Peter Kalm and others. Despite long and irregular passages of 18th-century ships, Bartram's plants got to England.

The trials, the successes and the failures, the prodding by Collinson, the constant patience and good nature of Bartram are recorded in a rich correspondence which flowed between the two between 1734 and Collinson's death. This is preserved in the *Memorials of John Bartram and Humphrey Marshall* by William Darlington (published in Philadelphia in 1849).

Evidence that Collinson's interest ran high is revealed by the requests which he piled upon Bartram in a never-ceasing number:

"Please to remember the Solomon's Seals that escaped thee last year.

"The Devil's Bit or Blazing Star, pray add a root or two, and any of the Lady's Slippers.

"The leaves of the Golden Rod are finely scented. Pray, have we any of the seed?

"Pray think of the fine new Laurel. We sadly want a specimen of it in flower. . . ."

But while Collinson was demanding he also had much concern for the well-being of Bartram. He sent books, found patrons and finally, on April 9, 1765, wrote, "I have the pleasure to inform my good friend that my repeated solicitations have not been in vain; for this day I received certain intelligence from our gracious King, that he had appointed thee his botanist, with a salary of fifty pounds a year. . . . Now, dear John, thy wishes are in some degree accomplished, to range over Georgia and the Floridas. . . ."

Some of Peter Collinson's suggestions for collecting and preserving plants were ex-

Franklinia, discovered by John Bartram in Georgia in 1765. Illustration from Charles Sprague Sargent, The Silva of North America, *Boston, 1891.*

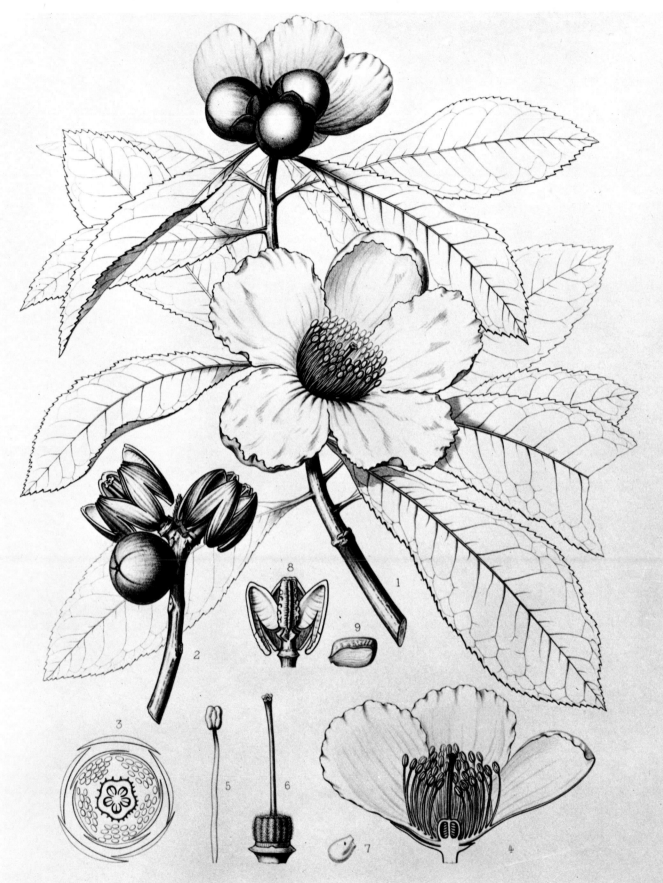

tremely practical. Perhaps he had a vague premonition of today's plastic bag and its usefulness to gardeners when he wrote on February 3, 1736, ". . . take thee three or four largest of ox bladders, cut off the neck high, and when a plant is found, take it up with a little earth to the roots; then tie up the neck of the bladder close round the stalk . . . [and] hang it to the pummel, or skirts of the saddle."

And on August 12, 1737: "Pray remember to send me the blossom and fruit of the Pawpaw in a little jar of rum. We never had yet a specimen of this tree in flower, and I want much to see the fruit, which will keep fresh in rum."

For shipping plants, Collinson wrote on January 24, 1735, "I wish, at proper season, thee would procure a strong box . . . collect half a dozen shrub Honeysuckles, and plant in this box; but be sure to make the bottom of the box full of large holes. . . . Then let this box stand in a proper place in thy garden, for two or three years, till the plants have taken root, and made good shoots. . . ."

The deep affection of Collinson for Bartram is evidenced in many warm passages.

"But these fine Lady's Slippers, don't let escape for they are my favourite plants. I have your yellow one, that thrives well in my garden.

"I congratulate you on so elegant a present, as the charming autumn Gentian. . . .

"March 20—Thy Columbine is in flower, which is earlier than any we have, by two months. It is a pretty plant, and more so for its earliness.

"I am in high delight. My two Mountain Magnolias are pyramids of flowers.

"I can't enough admire thy industry and curiosity in descending to so many minute rarities that came . . . [things] but what commonly escape the observation of most, but such a prying eye as thine."

John Bartram's name is closely linked with one of our most highly valued ornamental trees, *Franklinia* (or *Gordonia*). He first observed it in Georgia in 1765, and in 1777—the year of the elder Bartram's death—William, his son, brought seeds back to Darby. Twelve years later the plant was observed again in its natural habitat on the banks of the Altamaha river, but it has not been seen since, except in cultivation.

John Bartram's fifth son, William, was born on February 9, 1739. He closely followed his father's interests, and his excellent drawings of plants, plant parts and other natural objects, now in the British Museum in London, are important to the history of American flora.

That Peter Collinson was an important part of this history cannot be denied; Bartram and Collinson never met, but the latter's contribution to the knowledge of American plants exceeds any he could have made as a merchant of wool. We can be grateful for his persistence: "I have a sprig (in flower) of the Kalmia [mountain laurel] in water, and it stares me in the face all the while I am writing; saying, or seeming to say, 'As you are so fond of me, tell my friend, John Bartram, who sent me, to send more. . . .' "

Mountain laurel (Kalmia) was named by Linnaeus for Peter Kalm, who collected plants for him in North America. From The National History of Carolina, Florida and the Bahama Islands, *by Mark Catesby, published in London, 1771.*

Shakers and Sellers

"Fresh Garden Seeds of all Sorts, lately imported from London, to be sold by Evan Davies, Gardener, at his house over against the Powder House in Boston . . ." (advertisement, Boston *Gazette,* February 1719).

Cabbages and carrots are essential to survival, so in the days before supermarkets or even the great market gardens that once ringed our cities most families grew their own. Seed was gathered and saved from each year's crop to insure the next season's crop. For corn, peas and beans it was only a matter of allowing some of the ears and pods to mature, but for the biennials (carrots, cabbage, beets, turnips, etc.) two years are required to produce seed, so the matter was more difficult. Furthermore, while many kinds of vegetables can be grown to table maturity in Philadelphia, Charleston and Kennebunkport, conditions are not necessarily favorable in all three places to produce seed of all kinds.

As a result, in the earliest days, seed was imported from England, Holland and Germany and, as would be expected, seed trade centered around seaports.

The first major production of seeds in America did not take place until near the end of the 18th century when the Shakers began to do so at Watervliet and at New Lebanon in New York State. Later this production was taken up by other colonies in Massachusetts, New Hampshire and Pennsylvania.

The Shakers were the first to package seeds; they distributed them in their wagons to general stores in practically every town

B. K. Bliss & Sons, from their catalog of 1879.

204

and village. They allowed a 25 percent commission on all sales. At the end of each season they gathered up unsold packets to insure freshness each year. While their production was limited to vegetables and herbs —their faith restricted them to growing only "useful" plants—their products were of extremely high quality. In the first quarter of the 19th century the Shakers grew the best and probably the largest portion of the vegetable seeds in America.

Of the seed sellers, the first significant one was David Landrith, who established his seed house in Philadelphia in 1784. The store was located on what is now Market Street (near 12th) and a branch was soon established in Charleston, South Carolina, which continued until the Civil War. The Landriths grew some of their own seeds and operated a nursery in South Philadelphia. They are credited with introducing the zinnia to American gardens and were the first to offer the Osage orange, a thorny small tree which became a favorite for barrier hedges and which was brought to Philadelphia by Lewis and Clark.

The Landriths also sent a box of seeds to Japan with Commodore Perry in 1853 and received a shipment of Japanese seeds in return, thereby taking the first step in the importation of seeds and plants from Asia whence so many of our horticultural treasures come.

The contributions made by the great seed houses to American gardens—and to those abroad as well—are endless. The competition between companies has resulted in,

among other things, not only new and better marigolds and zinnias but hundreds of other improvements. Summer squash is no longer warty-skinned, large-seeded and "crook-necked"; instead it has a soft, buttery yellow skin, small seeds and a convenient straight neck. Asters resist "wilt" and green beans "rust." Sweet corn is sweeter, and when the principles of genetics which so spectacularly increased field-corn production in America were applied to petunias, new and wonderful ones appeared that Mr. Landrith would not have recognized.

It is not only for the seeds and the plants they produced that we must thank the seedsmen but also for the wonder of wonders—the seed catalog. Seed lists and catalogs appeared early, but the pioneer in producing the catalog with colored illustrations was B. K. Bliss of Springfield, Massachusetts and New York City, in 1853. Seedsmen were quick to see the advantages of mail-order selling.

Nothing breaks the gloom of a February day so well as does the arrival of the modern catalog, which excels not only in color but in superlatives. I remember with special pleasure the year I was eight years old; I invested every penny available in postcards to request seed catalogs. The marvelous avalanche that resulted continued for years. Large collections of catalogs in the libraries of Cornell University, the United States Department of Agriculture, the Massachusetts Horticultural Society and other societies and institutions provide a valuable record of plant introduction and use in America.

André Le Nôtre and the Family Mollet

Men sometimes seem to arrive at a time and a place in history which so uniquely suits them that it invites one to ponder whether man makes the time or time makes the man. Such a man was André Le Nôtre, landscape gardener. Also (from his epitaph): "Chevalier of the Order of Saint-Michel, Councillor of the King, Superintendent of Royal Buildings and Arts and Manufacturies of France, and Superintendent of the embellishment of the gardens of Versailles and other royal dwellings." To imagine the garden zenith reached in 17th-century France without the hand of Le Nôtre is nearly impossible.

André Le Nôtre was born on March 12, 1613. His grandfather, Pierre, had been a royal gardener at the Tuileries. His father, Jean, was also appointed a royal gardener and eventually became head gardener at the Tuileries, where during Pierre's time a member of the Mollet family occupied that position. At André's baptism, Madame Claude Mollet became his godmother. Appointments to the garden staff of the king were carefully protected and limited, so it was not unusual that three generations of Le Nôtres and what came to be a near dynasty of Mollets were associated not only with the Tuileries but with other royal gardens of France as well.

The Mollets—father, sons, grandsons—were a talented lot whose influence shaped gardens throughout Europe. Various Mollets served as gardeners to Henry IV and Louis XIII of France, James I and Charles II of England and Queen Christina of Sweden. That they came to be called "gardeners to kings" is not surprising. Two members of the family produced books that did much to spread their design concepts. Both were published in the mid-17th century, but Claude Mollet's *Théâtre des Jardinages* is considered to have been written about 1610 and was published posthumously.

André Mollet's *Jardin de Plaisir* was published in 1651. That the first book was written three years before the birth of André Le Nôtre and the second ten years before Louis XIV started to transform his father's small chateau into what became the palace of Versailles indicates not only the early activity of this extremely capable family but brings out the rich tradition and atmosphere into which André Le Nôtre was born. The foundation for what was to become the great French garden had been well prepared.

It was a Mollet who assisted in adapting the Italian idea of the parterre and refined it to become the *parterre de broderie*, the elaborately designed ground pattern which is so typically French. The Mollets planted *bosquets*—the great, planned groves of trees— and they developed the *patte d'oie*, the goosefoot pattern of radiating allées still existing at Hampton Court and in other gardens not only in England and France but throughout the Continent.

No other family so influenced garden design as the ubiquitous Mollets; yet to separate Le Nôtre from the Mollets is impossible, so intertwined were their private and professional lives. But while he may be a scion of the same tree, the products of his own talent were enormous indeed: Ver-

sailles, Vaux-le-Vicomte, Chantilly, Sceaux, Saint-Cloud, Rambouillet, Meaux and many others. The Tuileries as they exist today retain changes made by Le Nôtre as do many other parks and gardens large and small, public and private, throughout France.

The training of André Le Nôtre was not limited to horticulture. While he learned how to grow and propagate plants, to be sure, he also studied with a painter, learned to draw and obviously must have been more than slightly acquainted with geometry and engineering to enable him to shape the land as he did. The criticism sometimes leveled at his gardens as drawing-board exercises is grossly unfair because he used few architectural details and depended upon masses of trees, carefully planted and sheared, to create definition and confinement. Because of the year-around needs, flowering plants were gradually eliminated from the elaborate parterres in favor of carefully clipped boxwood combined with sand and gravel of various colors to define the pattern, yet the overall effect is that of plants rather than of architecture.

In the long section of the main axis at Versailles known as the *tapis vert,* the white statues and vases lining each side, although large in size and number, serve only to enhance and emphasize the walls formed by trees, the magnificent rectangle of lawn, the Grand Canal, the sky and the less formalized landscape beyond.

The great good taste of this man was reflected in the small house he and his wife occupied near the edge of the Tuileries where he collected paintings, marble, bronzes. About seven years before his death, Le Nôtre invited Louis XIV to view his collection and accept as a gift any items he wished to have. Among the 20 paintings the king selected were works by Poussin and Claude Lorrain.

Le Nôtre the man appeared to be as unique in his time as Le Nôtre the landscape gardener. The currying for favor, attention and position at the court of the absolute monarch was constant and intense, yet well-documented accounts of that court are consistent in presenting this greatest of gardeners as a completely plain-spoken man at ease with his king and with whomever he came in contact. From 1661 until his death in 1700 Le Nôtre was involved with the complex court and aristocracy of France; yet he carried out private commissions as well as those for the king. To the end Louis XIV treated Le Nôtre as a friend. In fact when the old gardener visited the king shortly before his death, Louis, already infirm, ordered two wheelchairs so that they could tour the garden, Le Nôtre being pushed beside his king as if of equal rank.

Much is made of the fact that while Le Nôtre moved among the nobility he never tried to be more than he was; yet he seems to have been respected by all. When Louis XIV ennobled him by making him Chevalier of the Order of Saint-Michel, Le Nôtre selected as his coat of arms a head of cabbage and three snails and answered his king, "Sire, would you have me forget my spade? Consider what I owe it."

Roses for an Empress

Wilfrid Blunt, in his wonderful book *The Art of Botanical Illustration* (Collins, London, 1950), separating the flower painter from the painter who paints flowers, states, "The greatest flower painters have been those who have found beauty in truth; who have understood plants scientifically, but have yet seen and described them with the eye and the hand of the artist." The line Mr. Blunt attempts to establish is a very thin one because there are painters who have captured all the freshness and fragrance of flowers without ever painting a petal as such and have, somehow, revealed truth.

On the other hand, there are some pedantic souls who delineate every dentate leaf and pollen-laden anther with painful precision and produce only dullness. Perhaps Mr. Blunt has chosen something to define that may be beyond definition. Yet there is an irresistible quality about good botanical (flower) prints.

A manuscript of Dioscorides, which dates from about A.D. 512 and is now in Vienna, contains drawings of such excellence that the plants represented are easily recognized. Yet for nearly a thousand years afterward plant illustration became so stylized that some, such as those in the *Grete Herball* (page 187) are almost worthless in terms of plant identification. With the coming of the "German Fathers of Botany," Brunfels and Fuchs, in the 16th century, plant illustrations became more natural in appearance and therefore more meaningful. Fuchs' herbal brought a refinement to woodcuts not usually associated with the technique (page 188). At the end of his work, he credits both artist and engraver.

The copperplate made a refinement possible which the woodblock did not. Exploration increased the flow of plants into Europe and the need to record plants increased. The discovery of new and useful plants was as much a reason for expeditions as were gold and conquest. In those pre-photography days an artist usually was included in expeditionary groups to record plants, birds, animals and other phenomena.

As sophistication grew, interest in plants increased to include the beautiful as well as those used for food, spice and medicine. The role of the botanical illustrator grew accordingly until, in 17th- and 18th-century France and England, this art reached its zenith. Great books were being printed: *monographs* to record a single genus or group of plants; *florae* to record the plants of a country, region or locale; or the less scientific *florilegium,* which is a book about flowers for flowers' sake, such as the spring-to-winter chronology of Crispijn van de Passe's *Hortus Floridus* (page 70) or an account of a single garden such as Besler's *Hortus Eystettensis* which records flowers of the garden belonging to the Bishop of Eichstätt, near Nürnberg (page 224).

Of all the illustrators, none reached the fame of Pierre-Joseph Redouté. The sheer quantity of his production is staggering; the beauty of it has seldom been excelled.

Redouté was born in France in 1759. His ancestors were Belgian artists and his two brothers became painters, too, so his talent was not without foundation. He visited Amsterdam and was much influenced by the Flemish masters and in particular by van Huysum. His first botanical illustrations were for L'Héritier, a French botanist, who published *Stirpes Novae* in 1784-85. This work contains 50 plates. Later Redouté illustrated succulent plants for the same botanist. Illustrations of succulents are of special importance because these plants do not dry, press and make good herbarium specimens.

Redouté also studied in Paris with the Dutch artist Gerard van Spaëndonck. Stipple engraving—a method by which a copperplate is etched by dots instead of lines —was being developed at that time. As a result a more subtle gradation of tone could be obtained and printing in color could be done from a single plate to achieve the softness and brilliance of watercolor. Van Spaëndonck developed a highly refined technique of painting with watercolor on vellum. This new technique when combined with stipple engraving (page 211) produced some of the finest prints of flowers ever made. Redouté (pages 210, 223) learned well from his teacher, for it is this technique upon which his fame was built.

When the Empress Josephine acquired Malmaison in 1798 she set out to create a garden which was to make horticultural history. Her love for flowers was such that expeditions were sent to all parts of the world for trees, shrubs, bulbs, herbaceous plants and seeds, but the flower she loved most was the rose. From China and Japan, from Persia, Turkey and Afghanistan, from all Europe and North America came roses of every kind. The collection became the turning point in rose history, and breeding experiments started there became the foundation upon which modern rose varieties developed.

Redouté came to Malmaison to record the plants of Josephine's garden. The *Jardin de Malmaison* (1803-04) contains 60 plates by Redouté. Between 1802 and 1816 he painted 486 lilies for *Les Liliacées*, which was dedicated to her, but his most monumental work is the record of the roses at Malmaison, *Les Roses*. For this he painted over 700 roses to create the largest single reference work to the rose species and its varieties. Unfortunately the empress did not live to see the work published (1817-24). She died in 1816; it can only be hoped that she saw at least some of the original paintings.

Pierre-Joseph Redouté died in his 80th year, on June 20, 1840. The years were not always good to him in terms of financial security, but he continued painting. His best paintings, on vellum, are in libraries and in private and museum collections throughout the world. Original editions of his prints can be found frequently. But the roses are everywhere: on greeting cards, note paper, reproduction prints, on wallpapers and fabrics. If you happen upon a moss rose in an illustration, or any other so-called "old-fashioned" rose, the chances are very great that it was first painted ever so carefully by Pierre-Joseph Redouté for his empress.

Rose, by Pierre-Joseph Redouté, *outstanding flower painter (print collection).*

Medlar, Gerard van Spaëndonck; first published in Fleurs Desinées D'après Nature, *c. 1800.*

Wilder and Hovey: The Pomologists

"The study of pomology, the collection of fine fruits and the planting of orchards," wrote Andrew Jackson Downing (Transactions of the Massachusetts Horticultural Society, May 1847) "have already become matters of very general interest and importance in the United States, especially in the Northern portion of the Union. Europe, and especially England, has already acknowledged the superior quality of American apples...."

The northeastern section of the United States still produces apples of superior quality, but the always brighter sky that Downing refers to, combined with temperature, rainfall and other favorable factors, provided excellent growing conditions for many other fruits as well. The Concord grape, many apples, strawberries, plums and peaches originated in New England. The search, development and introduction of them were the enthusiastic vocation and avocation of many men of the mid-19th century, but of none more than Marshall P. Wilder and Charles M. Hovey of Boston. In a leaflet announcing a lecture by Mr. Wilder before the Pennsylvania Horticultural Society in Philadelphia (April 13, 1871) he is credited for "importing many fruit trees... sparing no labor and expense to get new varieties, and at the same time distributing with a liberal hand the best varieties by trees and grafts."

So entwined is Marshall Wilder's name with the history of American horticulture and agriculture that it is met at almost every turn of the pages of the Victorian age. A wholesaler in West India goods and a merchant of domestic fabrics, Mr. Wilder's interest and industry involved him on a grand scale. He was a pioneer collector and hybridizer of camellias. He collected orchids; he was the fourth president of the Massachusetts Horticultural Society and an exhibitor of unsurpassed enthusiasm and generosity in its many shows. Mr. Wilder was a founder and first president of the United States Agricultural Society and of the American Pomological Society. The latter since its beginning has continuously been the foremost authority on fruit culture in America.

The variety of this man's achievements is endless, from the visionary to the down-to-earth practical. It was Marshall Wilder who first attacked the problem of the nomenclature of apple varieties. He found some varieties having different names in different localities and he found the same name applied to different apples. A Baldwin and a Roxbury Russet are after all not the same thing; agreement is essential to communication.

Of the professional horticulturists of the period, Charles M. Hovey of Cambridge acquired such fame throughout his achievements that he, too, was honored abroad as well as at home. A visiting Englishman, recognizing his prejudice against things American, admitted that the Hovey nursery was unique: "Entering by the gate you find yourself upon a fine, smooth promenade walk, about sixteen feet wide, bordered on each side by circular masses of exotic flowers;

Pear, from Duhamel, Traité des Arbres Fruitiers, *Paris, 1807-1835.*

directly in front of you stands a span-roofed plant house or conservatory, of Grecian construction. It is about ninety feet long and twenty feet wide. . . . In this nursery every sort of fruit is planted . . . not in dozens or even in hundreds—but in thousands. Everything in the trade is to be found here, as the proprietors spare no expense in securing everything they hear of, and a finer stock of fruit trees is not to be found, either in England or out of it."

Charles Hovey devoted many years to the improvement of the strawberry and in 1838 introduced the Hovey Seedling which was the first really good strawberry for American gardens. The fruits were larger, of better color and the plants more productive than varieties preceding it. At the exhibition of the Massachusetts Horticultural Society (of which Mr. Hovey also served as president), in which the Hovey Seedling was introduced, the judges called it "the perfect strawberry."

Hovey and his brother founded *The American Gardener's Magazine and Register* in 1835, which later became *The Magazine of Horticulture* and was continuously published until 1868. The writings of practically every important horticulturist of the period appeared at one time or another in the pages of this very popular journal. Charles Hovey also published two complete volumes and part of a third, entitled *Fruits of America*, which was issued in installments from 1847 to 1856. This work contains more than a hundred colored plates of many varieties of fruit sketched from nature by the talented Charles M. Hovey.

That the Hovey nursery gained fame is not surprising because even by mid-20th century standards it sounds impressive. The editor of the Boston *Transcript* reported in 1848: "...we were surprised at its extent and the immense variety of its contents. It comprises 35 acres of level, tillable land; and four greenhouses, each 84 feet in length. ...Of pear trees, it shows 1,000 healthy and beautiful specimens growing in avenues, embracing about 400 varieties; while, of these trees, in stocks and ready for purchasers, there are about 50,000. Of peaches, there are some 8,000 trees; of apples, 200 varieties, and 30,000 trees for sale; of plums, nectarines, apricots, cherries, about equal number....

"This is almost the only nursery in the country, where permanent fruit tree specimens, of full growth, line the avenues for miles. The effect is excellent. It is also a great satisfaction to purchasers to be able to see not only the infant tree but the specimen in its prime....The department of roses is particularly rich. Upwards of 800 varieties are here to be seen in full bloom. The whole neighborhood is scented with their delicious odor. . . . The fuchsias are abundant and large. The achimenes, gloxinias, and pelargoniums, the oranges, lemons, and cactuses, *that* immense Agave americana, . . . are all worthy of inspection. . . . We doubt if the visitor in Boston can pass an afternoon more pleasantly and usefully than by a visit to this spacious, well-stocked, and well-kept nursery of the Messr. Hovey & Co."

Papaya, from Plantae Selectae . . . *by C. J. Trew and illustrated by G. D. Eheret; published in Nürnberg, 1750-1773.*

a. *Flos hermaphroditus*, b. *flos femininus*, c. *fructus rudimentum* *discissum*, d. *calyx exiguus*, e. *semen pellicula sua candida adhuc inclusum*.

PAPAYA
ctu oblongo
lonis effigie
nef Infut. p. 629 Plum.
at. Specier. p. 20.

D. Jac. Haid. excud. Aug. Vind.

Repton and His "Red Books"

"Let us, then, begin by defining what a garden is, and what it ought to be. It is a piece of ground fenced off from cattle, and appropriated to the use and pleasure of man: it is, or ought to be, cultivated and enriched by art, with such products as are not natural to this country, and, consequently, it must be artificial in its treatment, and may, without impropriety, be so in appearance; yet there is so much of littleness in art, when compared with nature, that they cannot well be blended; it were, therefore, to be wished, that the exterior of a garden should be made to assimilate with park scenery, or the landscape of nature; the interior may then be laid out with all the variety, contrast, and even whim that can produce pleasing objects to the eye."

Thus wrote Humphry Repton in his *Fragments on the Theory and Practice of Landscape Gardening.*

Lancelot Brown had idealized the natural landscape of England until it could be idealized no longer just as André Le Nôtre had carried the French garden to ultimate geometry. In France Le Nôtre made the final statement, and reaction set in. So, too, in England after Brown, a change occurred. The most influential leader of the new approach was Humphry Repton, landscape gardener.

Repton came to his profession in a rather strange way. He had been well enough born (1752), educated and established in business by his father. When the business failed he retired to the life of a country gentleman waiting, it seems, for opportunity. He was well read, had skill as a writer and was talented with pencil and brush. One sleepless night in the summer of 1788, inspiration came to Humphry Repton and the next morning he wrote to several friends to inform them of his decision.

Humphry Repton built the bridge between the idealized park landscapes of Brown and the gardenesque that followed. Repton was responsible for the concepts that later became the Victorian garden.

Much of the success of Humphry Repton —who before his death became Sir Humphry Repton—was due, at least in part, to his skill with watercolors. It enabled him to make attractive before and after sketches of his client's properties. These were done with foldout sections of the sketches which dramatized the changes to take place. The delightful sketches were bound, along with written descriptions and recommendations, in red Moroccan leather and became known as Repton's "Red Books."

The "Red Books" alone became fashionable. Casually placed on a library table, a "Red Book" was a signal for guests to ask questions and provided a host with the opportunity to extol the wonders of his property (well supported by the "Red Book," of course) and then go on to describe the great potentials seen in it by Repton. By 1816 he had executed and presented over 400 of these books, and while over 100 gardens are recorded as works of Humphry Repton, it is safe to speculate that there were those who were more concerned about the "Red Book" than the proposals it contained. Such is the price of being fashionable.

Sir Humphry Repton impressed potential
clients with "before" and "after"
watercolors of their properties. Cut-out, hinged
sections gave dramatic evidence of the
changes he could achieve. From his Sketches
and Hints on Landscape Gardening, London, 1747.

Andrew Jackson Downing: Taste Maker

The mid-19th century was his time, the valley of the Hudson his locale, and "tasteful simplicity" was his plea. Born into a nursery operated by his father and later by his brother Charles, Andrew Jackson Downing learned to see not only the trees and bushes of his immediate surroundings in the nursery but the panorama of the whole valley. He learned well.

Few men have had so sudden and great an impact upon a population as did Mr. Downing. "I am still more anxious," he wrote, "to inspire in the minds of my readers and countrymen livelier perception of the BEAUTIFUL in everything that relates to our houses and grounds. I wish to awaken a quicker sense of the grace, the elegance, or the picturesqueness of fine forms that are capable of being produced in these by Rural Architecture and Landscape Gardening...."

Perhaps it was that the 1840s and 1850s were devoid of taste. But Downing changed all that by writing a book.

A Treatise on the Theory and Practice of Landscape Gardening was first published in 1841 and almost immediately became a best seller. Taste evidently had been born insofar as the occupants of the drawing rooms of Manhattan, the Hudson valley and much of America were concerned. By 1859 *A Treatise* had reached its sixth edition, by 1921 its tenth, and in 1967 a facsimile edition was brought out. Another book, *Cottage Residences,* brought about the Gothic revival: towered houses of quiet color (white was out!) to blend with the trees

and lawns of the "grounds." The furniture was Eastlake when it started, but it soon was turned into machine Victorian and Downing's cottages were bastardized until "tasteful simplicity" disappeared. But he cannot be blamed for what others did to his concepts or how they were later misinterpreted. Downing was an innovator.

"The development of the BEAUTIFUL is the end and aim of all other fine arts. The ancients sought to attain this by a studied and elegant regularity...the moderns, by the creation and improvement of their grounds which...exhibit a highly graceful or picturesque epitome of natural beauty.

"With regard to the literature and practice of Landscape Gardening in North America," Downing wrote, "almost everything is yet before us, comparatively little having yet been done." Perhaps that was true for the Hudson valley but, after all, Thomas Jefferson had built Monticello, George Washington had built Mount Vernon, and by 1840 there were impressive plantations in the South and a respectable garden or two on the outskirts of Boston and Philadelphia. Downing may have dismissed them because of the influence of the "elegant regularity" of the "ancients," but he did after all owe something to the English park, to "Capability" Brown, Humphry Repton and all who came before him.

In spite of what may at first appear to be geometry in the mid-20th century American garden, the value of landscape as composition and of plants as objects to be admired is perfectly compatible with his plea.

Frederick Law Olmsted: Park Maker

"The country—and such a country—green, dripping, glistening, gorgeous! We stood dumb-stricken by its loveliness, as, from the bleak April and bare boughs we had left at home, broke upon us that English May—sunny, leafy, blooming May—in an English lane; with hedges, English hedges, hawthorn hedges, all in blossom...." So wrote Frederick Law Olmsted in his *Walks and Talks of an American Farmer in England,* in 1852. American farmer he was but, more important, he was a man aware of the landscape, one who later revealed a talent for shaping it and a deep sense of how it should be made available for the enjoyment of all people.

When William Cullen Bryant and Andrew Jackson Downing joined voices in 1850-51 to demand a major public park for the city of New York, many listened. The issue had been bounced about for several years, but when the Common Council and the state legislature agreed upon a 150-acre site on the East River, Downing objected that this was much too small. Again people listened, and in 1853, the year after Downing's death, the site between Fifth and Eighth Avenues from 59th to 106th Streets was settled upon. Later it was extended to 110th Street—843 acres in all—to become Central Park.

Frederick Law Olmsted was born in Hartford, Connecticut, in 1822 and had had some success as a farmer and nurseryman, first in New Haven and later on Staten Island. His greater success up to this time, however, had been as a journalist. His re-ports of travels to the pre-Civil War South and to the West, published in part in the *New York Times,* became important historical documents. His *Walks and Talks* had drawn him to the attention of those whose love for the natural landscape also included concern that open space should be established for parkland in New York before it became too late to do so. It is not surprising that it was suggested that Olmsted might become superintendent of the new to-be-constructed Central Park.

When a competition was announced for a plan for the park, Calvert Vaux, architect and former partner of Andrew Jackson Downing, suggested that he and Olmsted collaborate. It was a difficult undertaking. Olmsted was at work clearing the new parkland of its shantytowns and other problems by day, so the plan was worked upon at night. The advantage was of course that as superintendent he had come to know the land thoroughly. The plan was entered along with more than 30 others. It won.

It was a long and hard road between plan and park, but as sections were completed and opened, public enthusiasm and pride ran high. Several concepts—such as the sunken cross arteries to keep traffic below vision and out of the way—were startlingly new to America and criticized severely.

In England, Olmsted had learned well from the idealized natural landscapes of Lancelot Brown and the gardens of Humphry Repton. The parks he refers to in his *Walks and Talks* are of course private landscapes: "...Probably there is no object of

Frederick Law Olmsted was severely criticized for his
sunken roadways and underpasses in Central Park,
designed to keep heavy traffic out of sight.
Board of Commissioners Report, *1860*.

art that Americans of cultivated taste generally more long to see in Europe, than an English park. What artist, so noble...as he, who with far reaching conception of beauty and designing power, sketches the outline, writes the colours, and directs the shadows of a picture so great that Nature shall be employed upon it for generations, before the work he has arranged for her shall realize his intentions."

He describes one such landscape, at Eaton Hall: "A gracefully, irregular, gently undulating surface of close-cropped pasture land, reaching way off illimitably; dark green in colour; very old, but not very large trees scattered singly and in groups—so far apart as to throw long unbroken shadows across broad openings of light, and leave the view in several directions unobstructed for a long distance. Herds of fallow-deer, fawns, cattle, sheep, and lambs quietly feeding near us, and moving slowly in masses at a distance; a warm atmosphere, descending sun, and sublime shadows from fleecy clouds transiently darkening in succession, sunny surface, cool woodside, flocks and herds, and foliage."

At a place called Birkenhead, Olmsted was urged to take the time to see a newly created public park. His comments about the manner in which the public used and reacted to this new concept were to be echoed later in the establishment of Central Park:

"...I was ready to admit that in democratic America there was nothing . . . comparable to this People's Garden...and I was glad to observe that the privileges of the garden were enjoyed about equally by all classes. There were some who were attended by servants...but a large proportion were of the common ranks, and a few women with children . . . were evidently the wives of very humble labourers....And all this magnificent pleasure-ground is entirely unreservedly, and for ever the people's own. The poorest British peasant is as free to enjoy it in its parts as the British queen. More than that the baker of Birkenhead [who had urged Olmsted to see the new park] has the pride of an OWNER in it."

Olmsted and Vaux evidently worked well together for, after Central Park, they went on to design Brooklyn's Prospect Park, Morningside and Riverside Parks in Manhattan, the original campus for the University of California at Berkeley and parks for Buffalo and Chicago. After the partnership ended in 1872, Olmsted moved to Brookline, Massachusetts, just outside of Boston. He is credited with designs for Mount Royal Park in Montreal, the National Capitol grounds in Washington, the Boston park system, Belle Isle Park (Detroit) and many others.

For his native city, Hartford, he designed 690-acre Keney·Park. I remember my own delight as a child there with the sheep meadow, well populated and straight out of the heritage of Lancelot Brown. In his *Walks and Talks* Olmsted reflects, "The sheep were of a large, coarse-wooled variety...but in groups at a distance, and against the shadows, far prettier than the deer...."

Tulipomania

The tulip had six pointed petals that were feathered delicately in patterns of violet and white. That it was lovely is hardly questionable, but it is hard to believe that speculation in tulips got so out of hand that the price paid for one bulb was:

2 loads wheat	2 hogshead wine
4 loads rye	2 barrels butter
4 fat oxen	1 complete bed
8 fat pigs	1 suit clothes
12 fat sheep	1,000 lbs. cheese
2 barrels beer	1 silver beaker

Tulips had not been in western Europe for many years when their popularity began to reach mania proportions—in Holland, in 1634. The first definite record of their coming westward is that of an ambassador to the court of Ferdinand I of Spain who brought seeds and bulbs to Vienna from Constantinople in 1554. A cargo of unknown size is reported to have been received by an Antwerp merchant in 1562. It is almost certain that these were not the wild tulips of Turkey but improved garden types.

Earlier in the century a Frenchman traveling in the Levant reports his admiration for the "red lilies" of Turkish gardens and goes on to state that they are "different from those which we have at home whose flowers are similar to those of white lilies." Since early tulips were similar to what is now called the Lily-flowering type with pointed petals rather than the square-petaled, boxlike flower form of the present-day Darwins, it is likely that the French-man was referring to tulips. Many scholars have maintained that these are also the "lilies of the field" in the New Testament.

Tulipomania was due to a biological characteristic of a particular type—the Breeder tulip—as well as the human weakness for gambling. Breeder tulips of the period were particularly prone to changing from a solid-color flower one season to a striped or feathered pattern of two colors the next. Such a horticultural freak is called a sport and is a permanent change which can be propagated vegetatively. Since tulips produce bulblets beside the main bulb each year, a desirable sport can be propagated with ease. If the flower was beautiful enough (and, as was the custom, you got enough friends to praise it in the tavern-trading houses) the bulb could have great commercial value not only for itself but for its potential offspring.

The mania, like most, began gradually enough as enthusiasm grew. Prices were going up among the connoisseurs, and of course legitimate dealers and producers of tulips were always alert for a new one. In 1623 a variety named Semper Augustus, which was feathered red and white and had a blue-tinted base, sold for "thousands of florins." As a result of such prices, and the fact that these accommodating Breeder tulips sported all by themselves, practically every man who could manage to plant even a few did so.

It was everyone's game: merchants and noblemen, seamen, chimney sweeps and mechanics. Property owners mortgaged it;

This lovely tulip with its "broken" color pattern is similar to those that caused "tulipomania." From Redouté, Choix des Plus Belles Fleurs . . . , *Paris, 1833.*

222

Tulipe cultivée (Variété) *Tulipa culta* (Var)

P. J. Redouté Langlois

Tulipa ex purpura rosea persica.   *Tulipa aurei colovis.*

V.

IV.   III.

Tulipa parte media viridibus   *Tulipa lutea prope calicem*
signaturis, altera vero rubra. *radis rubro.*

I.

Tulipa lutea maculis ru.

poor men suddenly possessed fine houses, coaches and horses. Wilfrid Blunt, in his delightful little book *Tulipomania,* reports that in one town alone over a period of three years the trading totaled more than ten million pounds sterling.

In the earlier days buying and selling took place between late June and September (from digging to replanting time) and the bulbs actually changed hands, but as the mania increased trading was carried on constantly, all year long. Speculators bought and sold bulbs they never saw nor even intended to see. At one point a contemporary wrote, "More roots were sold and purchased, bespoke and promised to be delivered than in all probability were to be found in the gardens of Holland." And since you really can't tell a tulip variety by its bulb, the chances for practicing fraud must have been irresistible. It was a great game; everyone made money. That is, as long as everyone played.

The stunning crash came in 1637. The amateurs and the speculators had tired of the game; it was all over. Delegates from various cities rushed to Amsterdam, lawsuits multiplied, but the jam in the courts made it impossible to get action. Finally the court of Holland decreed that a vendor could dispose of his bulbs as best he could but was allowed to hold the original purchaser to his contract and responsible for the difference between the contract price and that at which the bulbs were disposed of. But blood (or money) can be squeezed from tulip bulbs no more freely than from turnips, so many vendors settled for only five percent of the original price and were lucky at that.

The bubble had burst. Poets, social critics, cartoonists had a field day. Brueghel painted a neat town square bounded by fashionable houses and peopled with a crowd of tulip speculators. Their frock coats are elegant and the plumes in their hats are dazzling. But Brueghel made his point: all the figures have the faces and tails of baboons.

Holland has become the spiritual home of the tulip if not the actual one, and the enthusiasm of the Dutch—for tulips and business—has supplied the world with millions upon millions of these beautiful flowers. New hybrids are superior to old ones, are larger, cleaner in color and have the substance to stand up better to wind, rain, unseasonably hot sunlight and late cold spells. If you live where winter is too short, you can purchase precooled (artificially wintered) tulips. The mania has ceased, but the tulip has grown to a rank in garden popularity probably surpassed only by the rose.

In his . . . *Paradisus Terrestris* (1629) John Parkinson lists 140 varieties of tulips and states, "...all now made denizens in our Gardens, where they yeeld us more delight, and more encrease for their proportion,... than they did unto their owne naturals.... But indeed, this flower, above many other, deserveth his true commendations and acceptance with all lovers of these beauties, both for the stately aspect, and for the admirable varietie of colours, that daily doe arise in them...."

*One of the choice books of horticultural history records
the plants growing in the garden of the Bishop of
Eichstätt (near Nürnberg); illustrated by
Basilius Besler, 1613.*

EXHIBITION EXTRAORDINARY in the H...

Cartoon by George Cruikshank (1792-1878) *entitled* Exhibition Extraordinary in the Horticultural Room; *a meeting of the Royal Horticultural Society, London, January 1, 1826 (print collection).*

The Garden and Reality

Gardens are for philosophers, poets and lovers; they understand the reality of the forest of our origin. Garden is that forest, refined. The more complex the civilization, the greater the need for the garden, not only as an oasis but also as a reminder of our beginnings.

But gardens are also for mechanics and engineers, for dentists and draysmen and for politicians and shopkeepers, who might not be as aware of the garden itself as of the plants which are a part of it. Perhaps the attraction is based upon the fact that both men and plants are biological entities, more related to each other than to internal combustion engines, computers and lathes. Whatever the kinsmanship, man's interest in plants *per se* has existed since the first man created the first garden. His enthusiasm is often boundless; his purpose, difficult to define.

Take away modern hybrids and variants, which are man-made or propagated, and still the great majority of the ornamental plants which we use in our gardens, parks and street plantings grow naturally somewhere in the world. The fragrant lilac which is prized in one part of the world is a wild flower in another. Maybe the first garden lilac was the one that was moved from the wild to shade the doorstep of a man's hut. Then, perhaps, another man from the next valley where the lilac did not grow carried it home to plant by *his* doorstep. Why? Enthusiasm, fragrance, shade—perhaps the need was for something beyond words. From the new home in the new valley the plant traveled eventually around the world.

What but man's enthusiasm carried the common tawny day lily (Hemerocallis *ful-*

va) from China to Venice and Portugal (by Chinese-Arabian-Phoenician traders), then across the Atlantic to Philadelphia and Virginia and Massachusetts, only to be packed into Conestoga wagons and carried to the shores of the Pacific? Even today it grows along the route of the Oregon Trail where wagons were abandoned. In the Midwest it is often called "ditch lily" because of its habitat in ditches along roadsides that were once trails. The Chinese ate the flower buds and sometimes used the roots for medicinal purposes, but not the Europeans. The day lily was carried around the world merely because men liked it.

Collectors, breeders, propagators and growers have been responsible for bringing together vast quantities of information about plants based upon observation and experience. Many of the best man-made varieties of garden plants are the result of the work of the knowledgeable amateur, so while his obsession may at times appear amusing, his contribution has more lasting value than, say, the collection of baseball statistics.

The relationship of man and plants is a natural one. Both are real, and every place which is a garden, or is gardenlike, helps to preserve reality.

Opposite, above: Monographs of the 19th century grew so large they were lampooned, as The Orchidaceae of Mexico and Guatemala *by James Bateman, London, 1834. Below: Massachusetts Horticultural Society Flower Committee searching for heather in the marshes; from Vanity Fair, reproduced in* The Heather in Lore, Lyric and Lay *by Alexander Wallace, New York, 1903. Above: The perils of botanical illustration were many (Worthington Smith, sketching,* Gardener's Chronicle, *London, 1917).*

V. ONE BLOSSOM'S WORTH

Out of one wintry twig,
    One bud
    One blossom's worth of warmth
At long last

        Ranstsu (1653-1708)
        HAIKU HARVEST

Gardens are the most complex of the arts, for they deal with the organization of outdoor space within which all other arts are contained or take place. The Villa Lante and George Washington's Mount Vernon were conceived as entities, as two unified spaces inside which are contained buildings, pathways, pools, plants and all other materials and objects which meet man's needs and contribute to his comfort and pleasure. They are places *for* man. Garden is the art of *making a place* as opposed to just letting it happen.

In spite of those who fought for the picturesque, gardens are less related to painting than to architecture. Both architecture and gardens shape space to contain people. A painting is two-dimensional; it is only to be looked at but not entered into. Sculpture is three-dimensional, but until recently it was looked at only from the outside; when you move into the new sculpture, it tends to become architecture.

It is easy when studying gardens to be misled by two-dimensional plans, drawings, engravings and photographs which also emphasize the pictorial. From them it is nearly impossible to gain a sense of the space of the garden, of height and width and depth. While gardens such as the Villa Lante do have much in them that is pictorial, the primary quality is of organized space.

When James Rose said that being in a garden should be like being inside a piece of hollow sculpture he underlined the fact that the success of a garden depends upon the quality of its enclosed space. In order

to understand this concept, it is necessary to become aware of the volume of a garden and recognize our place within that volume. In this sense a garden is roomlike, but its walls, floors and ceilings are much more diversified than those of a room. The floors are lawn, paving, water, flower beds. The walls are hedges, foliage masses, fences, distant views, and the roofs may be arbor, vine, sky or overhanging branches of trees.

But in order to recognize the space itself, it is necessary to ignore, at least momentarily, the details of the confining structures

Preceding pages: North Philadelphia garden, Neighborhood Garden Association. Above: Carolina yellow jessamine, Wachapreague, Virginia. Opposite: Roof garden with awning of wisteria, Caprarola, Italy.

232

234 *Tree-of-heaven, Boston.*

Brook in winter, Hamilton, Massachusetts.

and materials. One can become enveloped in a garden composition just as in the composition of a great interior space. The excitement of being in a great cathedral comes from the shape of the enclosed space, not from the details of the floors, walls and ceilings.

The Abby Aldrich Rockefeller Sculpture Garden of the Museum of Modern Art in New York City is a place made for occupancy by human beings. Although it contains sculpture, the garden itself is also sculpturelike: it is exactly what James Rose must have had in mind. Man can move about within the volume of the garden and find it an exciting and dignifying experience. This garden is a *made place,* a delightful, comfortable and wonderful place. It is a bridge between the nearly completely artificial neighborhood and the natural world. It is also an extremely successful demonstration of how outdoor space can

become important in terms of human experience because of the direct action of man.

Another outgrowth of our approach to gardens as mere pictures has resulted in gardens having been hung on the wall, in a sense, and relegated to the decorative unnecessary. As a nation we have never considered gardens necessary. Yet Professor George E. Hutchinson, an ecologist at Yale, tells us that America is in trouble because "people can't sit in gardens, watch birds around them...." Professor Hutchinson is one of many concerned about the excesses of mankind. He has said that he thinks we will survive but warns, "...the cost to the satisfactions of life will be enormous. There is already a reaction to overcrowding in the cities—riots....We need more research not only on the minimal needs of people in cities but also on the optimal needs."

The most obvious is often least seen.

Above: Monarch butterflies on seaside goldenrod, Tuckerton, New Jersey.

Opposite: Gateway, Japanese house and garden, Fairmount Park, Philadelphia.

While we have been building bigger and faster and more automated cars, washing machines and can openers we have forgotten that human life is something that requires quality as well as quantity. The hardness of asphalt, concrete and steel is becoming increasingly oppressive. We are just beginning to learn that the need to sit under trees and watch birds is important for our mental and physical well-being. Science is discovering new relationships between living foliage and clean air. John Ruskin wrote, "I have never heard of a piece of land which would let well as a building lease remaining unlet because it was a flowery piece...." (*Modern Painters,* 1878).

If there is to be a tomorrow in which people can live as dignified human beings, there will have to be more land remaining unlet for "flowery pieces." Wilderness and national parks are important but so, too, are the city, the suburb and that awful no-man's-land in between which has been called the "Slurb." If the landscape is bad, it is because man has made it so. He can preserve a place, he can make a place—or he can destroy a place.

In the final analysis it is every man who makes the difference. Every man at some point in his life should plant a bean so he will come to understand that it is necessary to his sustenance. He should plant a tree to learn that it is necessary to his comfort, and he should plant a rose to learn something of grace.

Men make places, but places also make men.

Salt marsh with egrets,
Tuckerton. Succeeding
pages: Cornstalks in
Massachusetts.

*. . . Man's spirit cannot be shut off from
Nature and from beauty unless
civilization is prepared to pay a bitter
price . . . the worth of beauty is greater
than the passing pleasure it affords.*
Orville L. Freeman

The immortality of marbles and
of miseries is a vain small thing
compared to the immortality of a flower
that blooms and is dead by dusk.

Reginald Farrer

Illustration Sources

Acknowledgments

Bouquets are due to many:

Good friends listened patiently, and with their questions and arguments helped me to build the structure within which the story could be told. Among them are David Leach, Barbara Emerson, Reid Parker, William Frederick, Diane McGuire, Conrad Hamerman, Francis de Vos, Jan de Graff, Nelson Coon and George Lawrence.

The officers of the Massachusetts Horticultural Society who saw but the framework and encouraged me to continue: Oliver F. Ames, John O. Stubbs, George Putnam and Frederick S. Moseley.

And no small nosegay to the Society's librarian, Muriel C. Crossman, for her enthusiasm in the search for hard-to-find garden plates and prints; to George Cushing who photographed them.

And to my family—to Barbara who typed and retyped copy, to Stephen who worked in the darkroom for my photographs, to Peter and James who cheered us on, and to my wife who managed and endured it all as if it were everyday routine—I owe the largest bouquet of all.

Acknowledgment is also given for permission to reprint from the following:

Blake, Peter, *God's Own Junkyard,* Holt, Rinehart and Winston, New York, 1964.

Crowe, Sylvia, *Garden Design,* Hearthside Press, New York, 1958.

Beilenson, Peter, and Behn, Harry (translators), *Haiku Harvest,* The Peter Pauper Press, Mount Vernon, New York.

Miyamori, Asataro (translator), *Haiku Poems Ancient and Modern,* Maruzen Company, Ltd., Tokyo, 1940.

Pasternak, Boris, *Poems 1955-1959.* English version by Michael Harari, Collins & Harvill Press, London, 1960.

Rose, James, *Creative Gardens,* Reinhold Publishing Corp., New York, 1958.

Shepard, Paul, *Man in the Landscape,* Alfred A. Knopf, New York, 1967.

Index